The Constitution of Development

The Constitution of Development

Crafting Capabilities for Self-Governance

Sujai Shivakumar

THE CONSTITUTION OF DEVELOPMENT

First published in 2005 by
PALGRAVE MACMILLAN™
175 Fifth Avenue, New York, N.Y. 10010 and
Houndmills, Basingstoke, Hampshire, England RG21 6XS
Companies and representatives throughout the world.

PALGRAVE MACMILLAN is the global academic imprint of the Palgrave Macmillan division of St. Martin's Press, LLC and of Palgrave Macmillan Ltd. Macmillan® is a registered trademark in the United States, United Kingdom and other countries. Palgrave is a registered trademark in the European Union and other countries.

ISBN 1–4039–6985–X
ISBN 1–4039–6986–8

Library of Congress Cataloging-in-Publication Data

Shivakumar, Sujai.
   The constitution of development : crafting capabilities for self-governance / Sujai Shivakumar.
      p. cm.
   Includes bibliographical references and index.
   ISBN 1–4039–6985–X—ISBN 1–4039–6986–8 (pbk.)
      1. Political science. 2. State, The. 3. Political development—Case studies. 4. Economic development—Case studies. I. Title.

JA66.S46 2005
320—dc22   2005046427

A catalogue record for this book is available from the British Library.

Design by Newgen Imaging Systems (P) Ltd., Chennai, India.

First edition: October 2005

10 9 8 7 6 5 4 3 2 1

Printed in the United States of America.

In memory of my grandmother, Mrs. Parvati Jayasankar

Contents

Preface

What constitutes development? And how can the institutional basis for development be constituted? These puzzles emerged while assessing projects in Good Governance at the United Nations Development Programme's Regional Bureau for Asia and the Pacific in 1997. Having recently completed doctoral studies in Constitutional Political Economy from George Mason University, and believing that institutions matter, I wondered if the UNDP's initiatives in Good Governance could be effective.

I wrote of these puzzles to Vincent Ostrom, who invited me to pursue them as a visiting scholar at the Workshop in Political Theory and Policy Analysis at Indiana University. The following four years were spent attempting to understand the nature of development and—with an evaluation of aid, incentives, and sustainability for Sida—the political economy of development cooperation. This book is an attempt to draw together these understandings.

This book would not have been realized without Vincent Ostrom's guiding vision; his wisdom and steady encouragement resonate deeply. Colleagues and visitors to the Workshop in Political Theory and Policy Analysis also offered valued advice, and friendship. My thanks go to Krister Andersson, John Brown, Clark Gibson, Sam Joseph, Elinor Ostrom, Margaret Polski, and Amos Sawyer, among many others.

The book has benefited enormously from two formal manuscript review sessions. The first, held at the Workshop in November 2003 included Barbara Allen, Sheldon Gellar, Marilyn Hoskins, Minoti Chakravarty-Kaul, Michael McGinnis, Elinor Ostrom, Vincent Ostrom, Filippo Sabetti, Amos Sawyer, and James Wunsch. The second session, held at the Mercatus Center in March 2004, included Paul Aligica, Peter Boettke, Ken Borghese, Karol Boudreaux, S. Ramachandran, Gordon Tullock, Richard Wagner, and Fred Witthans, among others. My thanks to all for helping me improve this book, though its errors and shortcomings remain my responsibility.

Financial support for work on this book from the Workshop in Political Theory and Policy Analysis, Indiana University, and the Earhart Foundation is acknowledged with gratitude.

Finally, my family, especially my wife Ramā, has provided enormous moral support and encouragement, enabling me to persevere from initial drafts to the final publication of this volume.

Foreword

Some Contemporary Puzzles to Be Resolved

Sujai Shivakumar's *The Constitution of Development* is deserving of careful study and critical reflection. If we are to have a warrantable knowledge relative to the constitution of human societies, we need to understand the relationship of ideas to the thoughts and deeds that follow. The era of European imperialism came to a close after the Second World War with independent nation-states being created in much of the third world. Instead of achieving freedom for the colonial peoples, the new nation-states have frequently been the object of coups d'état by elements in the military who have engaged in pillage and plunder of their subjects.

Somewhat similar patterns occurred in the Marxist–Leninist revolutionary struggles to achieve the liberation of the working peoples of the world. The dictatorship of the proletariat yielded repression accompanied by profound tragedies, including mass starvation of millions of people. Concepts like capitalism versus socialism have failed to address the nature of exchange relationships and patterns of entrepreneurship in creating complementary orders in market and public economies.

A critical question that needs to be addressed in the twenty-first century was raised by Alexander Hamilton in the first paragraph of the first essay of *The Federalist* written in 1788: Whether societies of men are really capable or not of establishing good government from reflection and choice, or whether they are forever destined to depend for their political constitutions on accident and force.

Like the authors of *The Federalist* papers, Sujai Shivakumar in *The Constitution of Development* engages in a diagnostic assessment of the failure of unitary nation-states, explores alternatives, and conceptualizes the conditions necessary for the constitution of development confronting the peoples of the twenty-first century. This is why *The Constitution of Development* is deserving of careful study and critical scrutiny. The future of human civilization is likely to turn on the question of whether societies of men are really capable or not of establishing good government by reflection and choice, or whether they will continue to depend on accident and force. These are puzzles that you, I, and others must resolve.

Vincent Ostrom
Workshop in Political Theory and Policy Analysis
Indiana University, Bloomington

CHAPTER 1

Constituting Development

Development concerns the realization of our adaptive well-being through productive association with others. Institutions matter for development because they represent a shared understanding within a community of the rules we need to cooperate successfully with each other. Improving our adaptive potential requires that we recognize and renew these shared institutional resources to meet our current and future challenges in collective action.

Many assume that the "state" provides this institutional framework for development. Yet, the state—often conceived in the development literature as the preeminent locus for societal problem-solving—is prone to (and often does) fail in this institutional role. Addressing the challenge of development requires, therefore, that we advance beyond the framework of the state.[1]

Human civilization began with (and continues to depend on) our ability to govern ourselves through crafting institutions for social cooperation. Rediscovering the capacity for self-governance is essential if we are to foster and sustain our adaptive well-being. This book is an attempt to understand how we as citizens might constitute good government as the institutional basis for development.

Institutions and Development

Human development and economic progress correspond with the enhanced ability of individuals to improve their well-being through association with others. Successful collective action is required for individuals to do such things as grow adequate food, build roads, and maintain safe neighborhoods. Successful collective action is also required, more broadly, to craft and maintain the rules governing market exchange and collective decision-making. When the social technologies for collective action are kept in good repair, citizens are better equipped to solve problems, ensuring their current and future adaptive well-being.

People in all countries in the world face challenges of collective action. In the countries that we recognize as more developed, well-adapted networks of institutions generally lead to mutually productive outcomes. In poor countries, by contrast, individuals often continue to face incentives that make it difficult to invest in economic activities, provide public goods, improve communally held resources, and generally arrive at mutually productive day-to-day arrangements (de Soto 2000; Gibson et al. 2005). This failure of social cooperation is rooted in a variety of social dilemmas that, in the absence of countervailing institutions, lead to failures of collective action.[2]

The problem of "free-riders" and the "tragedy of the commons" refer to two common forms of social dilemmas. Free riders are those who seek to benefit from the actions of others without contributing their share of the effort.[3] As more seek to free ride on the toil of others, cooperation falters and the benefits of cooperation fail to materialize. The tragedy of the commons refers to a failure of cooperation in the shared use of a common pool resource.[4] In the absence of meaningful cooperation, individuals may be motivated to use more than their share of a limited but openly available resource, leading to its overuse and degradation. Failures of development occur typically when these and other problems of collective action remain poorly resolved. In fact, the characteristics we typically associate with underdevelopment—including widespread poverty, resource degradation, malnutrition, decrepit infrastructure, and crime—come to the fore when individuals in society fail to draw on, maintain, or even invent the various types of institutions required to solve basic, recurrent collective action problems.

Institutions are the prescriptions we use to organize all forms of repetitive and structured interactions (E. Ostrom 2005). They work by changing the structure of incentives individuals face in collective action situations and by creating shared expectations about the behavior of others (North 1990). In fact, we often recognize a culture or civilization as being so constituted because its members have, or had at some time in its past, crafted the institutions needed to solve recurrent problems of collective action.

For example, the institution of *ubudehe*, which existed in Rwanda long before the tragic genocide that occurred in the mid-1990s, helps solve a free riders problem. *Ubudehe* is rooted in a long history of inclusive community participation among the Hutu and Tutsi communities in tilling fields for planting crops before the rainy season (Government of Rwanda 2004). The concept of *xeer*, recognized among northern Somali pastoralists, is another example of a long-standing indigenous institution that, in this case, addresses potential tragedies of the commons. It encompasses a set of expectations concerning arrangements needed to share grazing and water sources among groups of nomadic herders who find themselves in a proximate area of rangeland (Lewis 1961).

The task of crafting such institutions is often complex and difficult because, in the real world, social dilemmas are numerous and frequently difficult to diagnose. Coming to agreement on new rules can also be contentious since individuals often have different theories about the working properties of proposed rules, as well as selective interests based on predictions of rule outcomes (Buchanan and Vanberg 1989). Yet, the very reality and, indeed, prevalence of institutions such as *ubudehe* and *xeer* in communities all over the world demonstrates that human beings are capable of recognizing problems of collective action and coming together to craft institutions in an attempt to resolve them.

Recognizing the importance of institutions, we argue that the issue of improving development requires a focus on the multiple contexts within which citizens can identify and craft new solutions to problems of collective action.[5] As we see in the following paragraphs, this institutional approach differs from traditional state-centered approaches to the challenge of development.

The State in Postwar Development

Development economics has long focused on the role of policies formulated and administered by a state to improve economic growth and human development (Stern 1989). This belief in the preeminent role of the state in fostering development gained particular strength in the period following the Second World War.[6] Based on what some considered the success of national planning in the reconstruction of Europe, leading theorists of the era posed that a similar rationalized approach would be successful in forging revolutionary changes in the developmental metrics of the countries of the third world.[7] The instrument of the state, it was believed, was unique in providing the necessary coordination and guidance required to the foster rapid industrialization.[8]

This rhetoric of state-led development was reinforced by what many in the postwar era saw as the promise of scientific economic management and professional administration. In that period, Keynesian models of the macro-economy promoted the belief that the business cycle could be tamed through fiscal and monetary levers controlled by a state. Neoclassical models of growth, advanced by Robert Solow (1956), saw the state as a key instrument to bring about the capital deepening and technological change needed for rapid industrialization. And the ideas of Max Weber and Woodrow Wilson convinced many that administrative unity along with policy coherence was needed to direct rapid economic and social transformations (for e.g., see Chenery 1971).

Driven by these circumstances, the economics and public policy literature that emerged in the postwar era viewed development as a transformation of societies from one set of circumstances—the pathologies associated with poverty, resource degradation, and malnutrition—to another possessing the trappings of a wealthy society, with the state as the prime agent for driving a constructive change. The legacy of this postwar approach to development continues today in key respects, not least in the endurance of major international development organizations founded in that era.[9]

The Limits of State-Led Development

This state-oriented framework for development has come under increasing scrutiny in recent times. Policymakers, aid practitioners, and scholars are increasingly questioning the effectiveness of traditional forms of development aid (see for e.g., Dollar and Easterly 1999; Burnside and Dollar 2000). At the macro level, aid inflows have been correlated with improved development metrics in states that anyway have better governance systems, questioning the additionality of aid. At the micro level, the poor sustainability of many aid programs has challenged the robustness of the development paradigm.

A major response to the challenge of aid effectiveness has been the focus on improving the potential of the state to use its development aid more successfully. The program of Good Governance promulgated by the World Bank and other aid organizations attempts to rescue the paradigm of state-led development by strengthening the capacity of third world states to generate good policies and establish effective administrative and adjudicative systems.

Civil conflict and terrorism reflect one of the more ominous pathologies of state failure. Liberia, Haiti, and Sudan are just some of the failed states that are synonymous with regional humanitarian crises today (Sawyer 2005). What's more, the dimension of state failure is rapidly evolving from regional to global. Terrorism spawned in failed states now threatens the security of the developed world (*The Washington Post* 2004; Eizenstat et al. 2005). Nation Building—involving the deployment of foreign troops to remove a regime and secure an end to conflict, the drafting of a new constitution, and the conduct national elections to legitimate a new state—is now the prescribed remedy for many dangerously failing states (Center for Global Development 2004).

Yet, initiatives in Good Governance and Nation Building will fail to be sustainable because they do not distinguish the *organization of a state*, often set out in a constitutional document, from the *institutional basis for good government*. National constitutions are often consonant with a hierarchical organization of government and a locus of power. Such formal constitutions will not foster an institutional basis for security and development unless they resonate with the common habits and understood practices through with individuals in those societies informally solve problems they variously confront.

A national constitution—even one that is avowedly decentralized in design—that fails to connect with these shared indigenous understandings is prone to foster instead a form of remote or centralizing governance—one where the rulers are estranged from the ruled. Such constitutions, however carefully drafted, are prone to become paper constitutions rather than living constitutions.

Basic problems of *knowledge* and *motivation* further limit the developmental potential of state-led governance. Statistical data, notably, do not capture the "knowledge of time and place," needed for a state's rulers to solve localized problems of collective action (Hayek 1945). And public officials, whose behavior is often shaped by incentives that inevitably arise within administrative and political hierarchies, can lack the motivation to search out better ways of solving social dilemmas facing the people (Wade 1985).

Moreover, an emphasis on state-led development can bring about, what Vincent Ostrom (1973) calls, "an intellectual crisis," in that it can stifle the development of a problem-solving political culture where citizens make efforts to work with others in their midst to craft solutions to shared problems of collective action. This culture of inquiry, participation, and problem-solving, crucial to good government, can be "trampled underfoot" by the ideology of the state, whose single and central power directly governs the whole community, noted Alexis de Tocqueville (2000) in his assessment of state governance in nineteenth century France. In such circumstances, observed Tocqueville, individuals cease to relate to each other as citizens of a problem-solving community and instead see each other as alike as subjects of the state.

The emphasis on the state-led development has indeed ruined capacities for locally based problem-solving in many developing countries—with catastrophic results in some cases. In Rwanda, for example, indigenous institutions such as *ubudehe* have been long overlooked in favor of (what was thought to be) the modernizing potential of a centralized government. The resulting deterioration of networks of trust, cooperation, and interdependence among the Hutu and Tutsi communities in favor of state-centric political identities have been cited as a factor contributing to the Rwandese genocide of 1994 (Mamdani 2002).

Successive Somali states similarly neglected the constitutional significance of indigenous problem-solving institutions. The formal constitution installed by the United Nations in 1962 expected Somalis to relinquish familiar clan-based institutions in favor of a new western-style parliament. Later, the Siad Barre regime officially banned indigenous clan-based institutions as backward, while exploiting rivalries among clan groups in a bid to divide and rule. Famine and civil war arose from this destruction of the constitutional fabric of Somali society, culminating in the collapse of the Somali state in 1991.[10]

These examples among others reveal that the widespread failures of development and humanitarian crises in Sub-Saharan Africa and elsewhere are rooted in institutional breakdowns—through neglect or even deliberate sabotage of existing indigenous problem-solving institutions by the state—and in the failure of state organizations to provide a viable and positive institutional alternative to the diverse challenges of collective action facing its populace.[11] State-led development, as Filippo Sabetti (2004: 14) sums up, is not tenable for three reasons: "first, because it looks to the national state or the Government as the only possible way to achieve and understand human order, equating it with modernity; second, because the argument rejects, or is insensitive to, the possibility that people can fashion and live under, multi-constitutional (or plural) systems of rule . . . ; and, finally, because it tends to identify democracy with the problem-solving and legislative capacities of parliamentary government and representative assemblies alone."

The Potential for Good Government

In *Democracy in America*, Tocqueville considered the issue of whether a society could be created where its members govern themselves on their own behalf, without recourse to the organization of a central state. He concluded that this would depend on citizens acquiring an "art and science of association" such that they could, at their own initiative, design, construct, operate, and modify patterns of associative relationships required to address their own adaptive needs. Tocqueville's purpose was not to commend the American model (and indeed, he found much wanting and even wrong about the United States) but rather to abstract positive lessons from observed best practices that could be applied then in other contexts—notably, the situation in his native France. Tocqueville is, thus, relevant for us today, not only for his method of institutional analysis, but also for his insight that the skill of citizenship, necessary for good government and development, can best emerge within a constitutional framework that is democratic and polycentric.

The Role of Democracy in Development

Although democracy is commonly associated with the idea of elections today, the term refers more completely to norms of inclusion in public discourse and decision-making—particularly those encouraging participation, debate, and consensus. In forums where citizens come together to solve local problems of collective action, participation helps ensure that such decisions draw on the knowledge that individuals have of their own time and place as well as on prevailing institutional understandings. Inclusiveness and consensus implicit in the broader meaning of democracy help strengthen common understandings about new decisions and rules. In this way, democracy helps create the institutional bases for successful collective action and, hence, development.

In his study of township government in New England, Tocqueville (2000) noted that the basis for a democracy, and the social stability and progress it afforded, rested in the shared beliefs and traditions of meeting, debating, and settling local affairs locally. What in turn made township governance effective, he noted, was that it drew on prevailing cultures of problem-solving, engrained in the indigenous traditions of its denizens. These mores, Tocqueville observed, created a basis for citizens to associate freely and to deal with public needs as they emerged.[12]

State governance, by contrast, rests on the expectation that others will provide good government. Democracy in this passive sense relates merely to voting for representatives to a national government. This political free riding, warned Tocqueville, can stifle a culture of local initiative and problem-solving so necessary for good government.

Polycentric Governance

In *Democracy in America*, Tocqueville further considered how local problem-solving institutions could form a mutually reinforcing network within a constitutional system. He found that while local concerns such as schools, roads, and public services were organized locally in the United States, these local efforts were constrained within basic rules set at the state level. In this way, governments at the state and ultimately federal level dealt not only with more broadly shared problems of collective action but also provided the parameters within which ongoing problem-solving efforts could be structured at the local level. In this way, if local problem-solving efforts within given rules were not successful, citizens could consider a change in the state or federal rules framing their own problems-solving efforts. This constitutional system thus provided a framework for problem-solving that was adaptable from the point of view of a citizen.

Tocqueville's account describes more generally a system of polycentric governance where overlapping arenas of political authority are present at various scales from local community organizations to national governments. Unlike state governance, which is hierarchical, polycentric governance is structured more as a network of networks.

In such a polycentric system, sovereignty is vested in citizens who, through processes of engagement within diverse though linked, institutional contexts, struggle to find solutions to their own common challenges (V. Ostrom 1999). The challenge of development is then one that we face as citizens in adapting new solutions to common problems within given institutional constraints as well as through crafting new alternative rules. Institutional regeneration through public entrepreneurship within a polycentric framework thus considers how well local institutions are adapted to the existing collective action situations, as well as to the way each of these institutions relate to each other.

Starting From Here

We have to "start from here" in constituting the basis for development.[13] The status quo itself comes about through choices made by innumerable individuals, each adjusting within multiple institutional environments. This activity creates a variety of outcomes, of which we may be able to discern particular patterns. James Buchanan (2004: 136) notes that "human action takes place within a set of rules, institutions, conventions, and practices that can be identified and defined. In this context, choice involves change from that which exists to something else." The challenge ahead is, thus, to identify and reshape prevailing institutions in an effort to create the patterns of outcomes consistent with improved health, security, and opportunity in human societies.

In this respect, a constitution for development differs from the postwar concept of the state as an abstract organization without reference to a status quo. Grounded in institutional realties rather than in ideology, the constitutional approach emphasizes that the future of effective development lies not in repairing or rebooting the state through Good Governance or Nation Building but rather in crafting adaptive systems of interaction—a constitution of development—that draws strength from and builds upon prevailing institutional understandings.

Building on Covenantal Foundations

For individuals to realize an improvement in their own welfare, the institutional arrangements within which they interact must be grounded in the local realities that inform their perspective and bind their community. Covenants, which imbue the citizen with the responsibility and moral commitment to struggle with others in recognizing and solving commonly confronted problems, take on significance in this respect (Allen 2005). These indigenous institutional resources need to be recognized if they are to serve as a foundation for renewed social cooperation. While differing in their cultural expression, such covenants are common to all civilizations. Olowu and Wunsch (1995) for example note that Africa's peoples have long provided for their needs and resolved conflict through indigenous African institutions and procedures.

A major challenge of development is to draw on these indigenous practices in crafting capabilities for self-governance. In this regard, a positive experiment is taking place in Rwanda today where *ubudehe* has been revived to foster collective action at the community level. Directed at the cellule level of the Rwandan government, *ubudehe* is being invoked to rebuild trust in communities torn asunder by genocide, to rebuild local institutions, and to encourage individuals to solve problems once again in association with each other (Dunbar 2004).

In Somaliland, the indigenous concept of covenanting or *xeer* has also been revived as a basis for crafting new governance structures. As described in chapter 10, in Somaliland, a network of institutional arrangements from the local to the national level that represent, in many cases, realistic responses to evolving civic problems is taking shape. While such developments give reason for optimism, we must also remember that the institution building process is long-term and inherently fragile. It is far easier to destroy institutions than build them.

Seeking Good Government

How can we build the context necessary to encourage individuals to craft and try new and locally relevant institutions governing collective action? And how can we reconcile each of the inevitable multiple and potentially contradictory and overlapping localized problem initiatives within a broader political economy?

Part I of this book describes how real world failures in development stem from an intellectual crisis related to the concept of state itself. It describes why the idea of a unitary state—one that has asserted itself in the literature and practice of development from the postwar period to the present—limits the creative potential of individuals to improve their mutual well-being through crafting capabilities for self-governance.

Part II argues that development results from a citizenry possessing the capability for crafting rules for collective action and from individuals realizing the benefits of social cooperation. Institutional problem-solving concerns not only specific interactions but also more broadly, the set of understandings underpinning broader market and non-market interaction.

Finally, Part III reconciles the reality of multiple and overlapping arenas of collective action within a system of polycentric governance. It describes how individuals, by drawing on available institutional resources, can rediscover the institutional artisanship necessary to realize their adaptive well-being.

Civilization arose as human beings developed increasingly complex and yet adaptable systems of social cooperation. If we are to realize a democratic civilization in the twenty-first century, we need to identify and understand the principles applicable to successful collective undertakings across time, geography, and language. The challenge of Constitutional Political Economy lies in looking beyond the ideology of state governance to understand the nature of collective undertakings with reference to multiple levels of governance and multiple sources of adaptation.

PART 1

State Governance and Development

CHAPTER 2

Postwar Interpretations of Development

What is at stake is nothing less than whether human beings can act, collectively, to improve their lot, or whether they must once again accept that it is ineluctably determined by forces over which they have, in general, little or no control.

Colin Leys, *The Rise and Fall of Development Theory*

Pathologies identified with underdevelopment arise when existing weak or bad institutions fail to address recurrent localized problems of collective action. Development theory and aid practice in the western postwar tradition focus predominantly on the overall outcomes of these institutional failures, assigning to the state a central role in fixing these negative results. An alternate vision is to examine why institutions fail in the first place. This broader notion places emphasis on improving the innovative potentials of humans to develop and maintain the institutions needed to overcome problems of collective action. Developing this alternate vision is the larger aim of this book. In placing constitutional governance in context, this chapter examines some links between postwar interpretations of development with the approach of state governance.

The Context of Postwar Development

The concept of "development" remains caught up in many ways in a special meaning, taken up in the *zeitgeist* of the postwar period, when western leaders perceived a pressing need to secure geopolitical alliances in Europe against the emerging cold war with the Soviet Union.[1] Shortly after the Second World War, an important concern of the United States leadership was the reconstruction of

Europe. This concern, with its strong emphasis on capital formation, colored thinking about the nature of development.

Postwar development theorists also placed a strong emphasis on national economic planning, which called for the state to play an instrumental role in resource allocation.[2] Wartime economic policies had relied heavily on national planning by the state, and policies framing national reconstruction that followed the war also directed governments to take the lead in rebuilding the physical infrastructure destroyed by the war.[3] The idea of state-focused development, based on an emerging Keynesian Political Economy, appeared to meet these exigencies (Browne 1999). An idea that seemed reasonable at that time, it provided a framework for concrete action in a world otherwise torn upside down by war and ideology.

Referring to the appeal of Keynesian Political Economy, Milton Friedman (1999) has noted that "Keynes believed that economists (and others) could best contribute to the improvement of society by investigating how to manipulate the levers actually or potentially under the control of the political authorities so as to achieve desirable ends and then persuading benevolent civil servants and elected officials to follow their advice." This paternalistic view, he notes, was more persuasive to economists and policymakers than Hayek's warnings in *The Road to Serfdom* of the potential for tyranny in a paternalistic state.[4]

Another major postwar development shaping the meaning of the term development emerged in the context of a need—particularly by Great Britain and France—to structure continuing economic and political relationships with their newly independent former colonies. Concurrently, leaders of newly independent states were seeking to cultivate a sense of national unity among disparate communities juxtaposed within the legacy of often arbitrary colonial boundaries. The mission of development, with the state leading this effort, provided a raison d'être for the state.

India, like many other newly independent states at the time, faced critical shortages of basic infrastructure. What physical infrastructure existed—the railways, for example—was of British origin and required parts from Britain to keep in running order. Similarly, parliamentary and administrative systems in India were of British design. To the extent that India (like other new states) was a colonial invention, its new rulers had to maintain the core physical and institutional networks that had bound its diverse cultures together within a single identity.[5] For Prime Minister Nehru, state-led national development, inspired in part by the apparent success of the Soviet planning model, fitted this need to maintain national coherence.[6]

Taken together, a theory of third world development that looked to a device called the state arose in response to the exigencies facing both donors and recipients in the postwar period. It was based on the idea of states providing developmental assistance to other states, where the state was construed to be the prime agent in promoting national objectives in social and economic transformation. In a world turned upside down on a global scale, the idea of state-directed development appeared to provide a practical way forward.

Some key features of this emergent postwar framework of development are highlighted in the following paragraphs.

Development as Transformation

Postwar development economics frames a specialized area of inquiry and application concerning the problems facing the world's poor countries. Its rhetorical orientation is to reduce rates of poverty in these countries and to improve national potentials for economic growth and human development.[7]

As the field of development economics has grown over the past fifty years and more, it has referred to specialized meanings of development and the role of the state in this development. Development, in this postwar context, relates to a transformation of societies from a primitive stage to an advanced stage, principally through capital formation.[8] This notion later gave way to the idea of development as transformation with the modernization theories of the 1960s (Seers 1969; Haq 1972). As Joseph Stiglitz (1998) put it more recently, "Development represents a *transformation* of society, a movement from traditional ways of thinking, traditional ways of dealing with health and education, traditional methods of production, to more 'modern' ways." The role of the state[9] in development is as the agent of change—it is a device to fix market failures and resolve social dilemmas.[10] Even some so-called institutional approaches rely on the state as the organizational context for implementing development (see for e.g., Israel 1987; Killick 1995).

Scorecards of progress in this transformative development are provided by national statistics, aggregated at the level of the state. These measures of growth, literacy, gender equality, and the like, appear to enable the comparison of less developed states with more developed ones.[11] The *World Development Report* published by the World Bank and the more recent *Human Development Report* of the United Nations Development Programme (UNDP) report such data annually. A lack of progress in these league tables is often seen as a reflection of a country's failure to develop.

The Role of Development Assistance

Another significant feature of postwar development is the system of state-oriented development assistance—often referred to as aid. Aid emerged as a key instrument to continue many of the international linkages in trade and production previously subsumed within colonial relationships. Referring to the African experience, Cooper (1997) notes that, with the end of empire, Britain and France sought a new framework for maintaining mercantile relationships with their erstwhile colonial possessions.[12] With their own economies still dependent on imperial patterns of trade, a particular rhetoric of state-directed development, based on the framework of Keynesian Political Economy, emerged to reestablish control over the agendas of the rulers of newly independent states. This framework placed emphasis on policymaking and administration by the rulers of a state.

As already noted, aid also served to secure strategic alliances with the rulers of poor countries in the cold war standoff. Aid to states, often with emphasis on military capabilities, was a key tool in the new crypto-imperialism, securing loyalties in the postwar geopolitical order (V. Ostrom 1988). Here too, Keynesian Political Economy provided the necessary rhetoric, reinforcing the use of power by friendly rulers over their states.

Official aid agencies—postwar inventions—were chartered on the premise that the citizens of a donor state (or a collection of donor states) could provide the agents of a recipient state with resources and policy advice needed to carry out particular development objectives (Krueger 1998). Today, large and well-resourced international aid organizations continue to dominate the development landscape. Highly visible multilateral organizations include those of the World Bank, the various development agencies of the United Nations, and the European Development Fund.[13] Influential bilateral agencies include the United States Agency for International Development, France's "Direction générale de la Coopération internationale et du Développement," the British Overseas Development Agency, and the Swedish International Development Agency. Official aid is conducted via the agents of the recipient state.

These aid organizations have shaped the evolution of development economics in important ways, having sponsored much of the postwar literature on development economics. Given their specific missions, they have promoted approaches to development that fit with their own organizational constraints. Today, aid is nearly synonymous with development. As P.T. Bauer (1984: 155) notes, development economics "owes its existence to the concept of underdeveloped countries, which in turn is derived directly from a particular policy, namely the policy of foreign aid." The built-in relationship between development theory and development assistance is a hallmark of postwar development.

Aid has been more successful in nurturing development in cases where the scale and the nature of the particular collective action problem faced by individuals in a recipient country are suited to the approach to development of the postwar framework (Cernea 1987). Research and international cooperation made possible by aid have, for example, spawned the Green Revolution and eradicated the smallpox virus.[14] Within smaller, more specific contexts, aid programs and projects have also been of benefit to poor communities throughout the world (Ostrom et al. 1993).

In many cases, however, the development interventions have not been sufficiently sensitive to the prevailing problems of collective action that gave rise to the need for aid in the first place. Moreover, aid has often exacerbated prevailing institutional asymmetries (Gibson et al. 2005). Official aid, which is channeled through the agents of the recipient country, often strengthens the power of developing country rulers over their subjects. Indeed, rulers of aid-dependent states are often found to be less responsive to their own people than are rulers of more aid-independent states (Bräutigam and Botchwey 1992). In this way, aid can mask a control apparatus behind a veil of rhetoric about growth and human development.[15]

Bridging Gaps and Fixing Failures

A third interrelated fixture of the postwar development mind-set is its focus on state intervention to repair impeding failures. Early on, Samuelson (1954) and Bator (1958) highlighted *market failure*—pointing to under-produced public goods, high transaction costs, and egregious externality problems that characterize many developing countries—and recommended that the state rectify them. W. Arthur Lewis (1954), Evsey Domar (1957), and W.W. Rostow (1960), among others, also identified critical deficiencies in essential physical and financial infrastructure as impediments to growth in developing countries, recommending that aid from developed to developing states fill in these critical gaps.

Institutional failures, stemming from social dilemmas, characterized variously as the Prisoner's Dilemma, the Tragedy of the Commons (Hardin 1988) and the Logic of Collective Action (Olson 1965), have further been proffered to explain often observed patterns of human exploitation and resource degradation in developing countries. The postwar development response, again, looked to intervention by reasoned policies administered by the state to resolve such dilemmas (Ophulus 1973).

By the 1980's, development failure was linked increasingly to *government failure*. Scholarship in Public Choice pointed out that rent seeking and rent-avoidance activities, occasioned by excessive discretion on the part of the agents of the state, foster waste and retard growth (Tullock 1967; Krueger 1974; Bhagwati 1982). Responding to this, development theorists recommended aid to improve the organizational capacity of the state. The idea of Good Governance was soon invoked by the World Bank and the UNDP to overcome the problem of government failure (Kaufmann et al. 1999).

In all, development theory in the postwar tradition advocates state action to transform societies, assisted by donor funds and expertise. This view has been challenged by findings that this international development assistance has had, despite notable individual successes, no statistically discernable positive aggregate effect on growth.[16] The term, "aid failure," which has since entered the lexicon, is linked to the prevalence of poor policy environments in recipient governments (Collier 1999; Dollar and Easterly 1999; Dollar and Svensson 2000).[17] Recent fixes, including aid conditionality and Sector Wide Approaches attempt to use donor aid as a lever to encourage and facilitate the adoption and administration of appropriate policy recommendations by agents of recipient states.

Development theory has focused on the modernization and transformation of poor societies through state-based governance. It continues to be largely oriented toward providing a ruler with advice on how to deal with the problems of underdevelopment. Fixes for market failures and social dilemmas turn to the state as the corrective mechanism. Fixes for government failure also turn to the state to correct this deficiency. The role of aid is to provide the state with the necessary wherewithal, access to technical competence, or the political cover, to carry out these tasks.

Recasting Development

Karl Popper (1971) in *The Open Society and its Enemies* noted that conceptually simple devices that promise to take care of very real human needs are often delusions that lure societies into totalitarianism. Plato's philosopher king, Hegel's state, and Marx's dictatorship of the proletariat are all shorthand abstractions that promise to fix problems in society. However appealing, these prescriptive forms are prone to yield large and counter-intentional institutional dimensions with egregious consequences for liberty and well-being, concluded Popper.

The focus of postwar development similarly relies on an elementary concept—the state—as the device to eradicate poverty, hunger, and disease in the poor countries of the world. Yet, a theory of development that advises the ruler of a state to take appropriate policy action on behalf of his people and a system of development aid that strengthens the hand of this ruler against others so that he may do good, leads to a constitutionally unbounded state. As we examine further in Part I of this book, such an unbounded state is more prone to shut off meaningful civic participation, more prone to exhibit predatory behavior, and thus more prone to fail to develop and maintain institutions needed to cope with problems of collective action. If the putative role of the state is to reduce poverty, hunger, and disease, the promise of such development can be vitiated by the unbounded nature of the state itself.

Indeed, several aspects of the postwar development infrastructure have been increasingly questioned in the literature. Leys (1995) account of the fall of development theory and Browne's (1999) analysis of the demise of development assistance point, for instance, to defects in a framework of analysis that largely neglects the institutional context of human action.

Moreover, the idea of development-by-state, born of a system of international relations made necessary in the immediate postwar period, has itself been over-taken by events: the cold war has ended and new patterns of regional and global economic and political integration have arisen.[18] Official aid, conducted by multilateral and bilateral aid organizations, has been eclipsed in many cases by direct foreign investment as well as by unofficial aid in the initiative of numerous nongovernmental and civil society organizations (OECD 2001).[19] Finally, and not least, numerous analysts have challenged the effectiveness of aid, as we review in the next chapter. These events, in themselves, call for a reevaluation of our understanding of the present infrastructure of international development assistance and prompts further introspection of what constitutes development and how to constitute development.

CHAPTER 3

The Aid Effectiveness Puzzle

With Krister Andersson, Clark Gibson,
and Elinor Ostrom

R esearchers and public officials trying to improve economic performance in the postwar period believed that the core problem of development was the lack of sufficient monetary resources needed to build necessary physical infrastructure and to enhance investment in local economies (see Rostow 1960; Prebisch 1970; Huntington and Weiner 1987). If the problem was one of "missing money," the proposed solution was to "send money."

Had this diagnosis had been correct, the billions of dollars that donor countries have allocated to developing countries over the last four decades should have gone a long way toward solving the problem of underdevelopment (Van de Walle and Johnston 1996). To be sure, many individual infrastructure, health, and educational projects have had notable successes (e.g., Bosc and Hanak-Freud 1995; Maipose et al. 1997). Nevertheless, there is growing evidence that sending money has not substantially reduced the relative poverty levels of most recipient countries (Krueger et al. 1989; Blomstrom and Lundahl 1993). In some African and Asian countries, poverty has become more severe today than it was half a century ago (Boone 1996). Even in countries that have experienced some growth, the lives of the poorest members of society have often remain unchanged or even deteriorated (Elgström 1992).

This aid puzzle challenges us to look more deeply at the nature of development.[1] In this chapter, we consider that failures and successes in development are rooted in failures and successes in collective action. Here, development can be understood as a process where individuals, through the design and use of institutions at many scales, increase their well-being by identifying and solving collective-action problems more effectively. Development aid that fails to address these underlying collective action problems will likely remain ineffective.

The Challenge of Aid Effectiveness

The postwar development model has been under increasing scrutiny, with policymakers, aid practitioners, and scholars calling into question the effectiveness of development aid to increase economic growth, alleviate poverty, and promote social development. A number of macro-level studies in the 1990s found little consonance between aid levels and desirable changes in macro-level indicators (Pack and Pack 1990; White 1992; Boone 1994; Devarajan and Swaroop 1998; Feyzioglu et al. 1998; World Bank 1998; Dollar and Svensson 2000; Burnside and Dollar 2000a; Easterly 2002b, 2003). Aid programs at the micro level have also often found to fail (Elgström 1992; White 1992, 1998, 1999; Catterson and Lindahl 1999). While not all macro assessments have been negative (and many micro assessments remain positive), the widespread perception of aid ineffectiveness continues to challenge both aid agency officials and scholars.[2]

Responding to this evidence, donor governments and multilateral financial institutions have begun to demand new, more productive delivery systems for aid. As a result, new concepts have emerged in vocabulary of the post–cold war development aid agencies, including "sustainable development," "recipient ownership," and "aid conditionality" aimed at improving aid effectiveness.[3]

"Sustainable development," as defined in the Brundtland Report, "seeks to meet the needs and aspirations of the present without compromising the ability to meet those of the future" (WCED 1987: 40). The term, however, has taken on many interpretations in the context of development aid. A recent effort to examine (and measure) sustainability led Bell and Morse (1999) to conclude that the concept's myriad usages ranged from an empty slogan to a loaded normative term used primarily for political purposes. For development projects, sustainable development often means that the positive impact of an aid project continues beyond the direct involvement of the donor—an interpretation that is more closely associated with the idea of aid effectiveness.

Such sustainable development often requires greater participation or "ownership" by aid recipients. This shift implies a concomitant decline in a donor's authority over their own aid packages as well as a greater responsibility on behalf of the recipient (OECD 1992; Johnson and Wasty 1993; Brunetti and Weder 1994; Wilson and Whitmore 1995; Van de Walle and Johnston 1996). Without such ownership, some argue, recipients will not make the kind of commitments needed to ensure the realization of the intended long-term results of donor assistance. A failure by donor agencies to push the type of institutional development that increases the ownership capabilities of the beneficiaries, they argue, risks a continuation of the type of unsustainable development aid that has characterized much of recent experience.

Ownership has thus become an important and fashionable concept among many development assistance agencies in the world today.[4] And yet the meaning of ownership remains unclear, especially when confronted with the reality of development ownership in the field. Donor agencies and their contractors, for example, exert many of the prerogatives of ownership while the target beneficiaries often remain passive participants in aid delivery (Gibson et al. 2005). As Bräutigam (2000: 32) notes, the question of what "ownership" means in development assistance is not clearly answered either by the scholarly literature or by the donor agencies themselves.

Another key arrangement designed to improve aid effectiveness is the idea of making aid delivery conditional on policy and administrative performance by the recipient government. Conditioning aid in return for explicit negotiated commitments to reform means that policy change is the price that recipient governments pay in exchange for aid. Collier (1999) explains why such conditionality can fail to improve aid effectiveness, pointing out for example that if a donor "buys" reforms with aid, it becomes, in effect, the owner. Indeed, *ex ante* conditionality is widely seen to have failed as a tool to improve aid effectiveness (Stiglitz 1999). At the same time, the administration of *ex post* conditionality, which seeks to reward recipient rulers seen to be more responsible stewards of their state with aid (Gilbert et al. 1999), often conflicts with donors' commercial and geopolitical motivations for providing aid and, given an understanding of the institutional context of development (discussed in the following paragraph), also raises questions about the central focus on aid in the development puzzle.

The Institutional Contexts of Development

Rather than simply blame corruption (whether on the part of donors, the private sector, or recipient governments), some analysts have shifted their focus toward the institutional settings of aid (Martens et al. 2002). According to this view, the poor outcomes associated with aid do not need conspiracies to flourish, but are quite predictable given the preferences of the individuals involved and the incentives generated by the way in which the institutional contexts of development are themselves structured. Their work argues that no matter how well-intentioned those providing assistance are, or how many resources are transferred, development will occur only if political and economic institutions generate incentives that facilitate individuals' achievement of development goals.

This recognition requires that we more carefully examine the role of institutions and consider how we can analyze institutions.

The Meaning of Institutions

Institutions are the rules that individuals use in a wide diversity of repeated situations confronted in life. The rules that individuals adopt, along with other contextual factors directly affect their incentives and consequently the likelihood that they will achieve higher levels of productivity in the many collective-action situations faced in everyday life. Thus, institutions help or hinder the efforts of individuals to be optimally productive in the activities they undertake with others.

A key aspect of all institutions is a shared understanding of the rules within a community regarding what actions individuals must take, must not take, or are permitted to take in particular settings (Crawford and E. Ostrom 1995).[5] These prescriptions are the rules of the game that coordinate human interaction. They "structure incentives in human exchange, whether political, social, or economic" (North 1990: 3). Rules of the road, for example, reduce the potential for chaos by solving basic problems of traffic coordination.

However, not all institutions are positive. Working rules may come about "informally" to serve illegal or immoral purposes. For instance, institutional arrangements among politicians, allowing them to behave as organized bandits (McGuire and Olson 1996) and prey on the citizens, do not promote the overall prosperity of societies. In some bureaucratic organizations, officials have set the price that must be paid by an applicant in order to receive a position in the bureaucracy (Wade 1985). Here, the rules by which positions are to be purchased are well known, as are the rewards and punishments for observing or violating these (usually illegal) rules and norms. Although such rules and norms create incentives that promote cooperation and coordination within the rent-seeking bureaucracy, the corruption and ineptitude sponsored by this institution inhibit the development of the larger society (de Soto 2000).

Analyzing Institutions

The Institutional Analysis and Development (IAD) framework, developed by scholars affiliated with the Workshop in Political Theory and Policy Analysis at Indiana University, presents a practical method for deconstructing institutions.[6] It enables the investigation of complex and interactive processes characteristic of action arenas in development.

IAD distinguishes between three levels of nested rules and interactions. At the day-to-day or *operational* level, it views individuals interacting in repetitive settings that directly affect physical outcomes. The rules that affect the structure of an operational situation are themselves designed and agreed upon in *collective-choice* situations. Policymaking, in this context, is often associated with elected officials in legislative or executive bodies who make decisions about rules that affect the structure of many operational situations, although indigenous forums for policymaking found in developing countries can be as (or even more) apposite. These policies are themselves framed within formal and informal *constitutional* rules that affect the issue of who will make policy decisions using what type of rules and procedures.

IAD also highlights the working rules, biophysical or material conditions, and community attributes that provide the initial conditions or "the environment" that structure efforts to achieve outcomes. It is within these parameters that an analyst can identify an *action arena*, which is composed of the incentives generated by the situation's context, and the incentives of the particular actors involved. Ultimately, it is these actors, operating within the incentives produced within action situations, who interact and make choices that generate tangible outcomes.

A key concept in IAD is that of a *collective-action situation*, which occurs whenever a desired joint outcome requires the input of several individuals. Such collective-action situations lie at the core of development. Indeed, almost all productive relationships involve some form of collective action. For example, while one person can farm a single, small agricultural plot, his or her productivity is greatly enhanced by creating diverse forms of teamwork through family, community, or corporate arrangements. Similar benefits of increasing the number of participants who bring different skills and resources occur in almost all manufacturing or service activities.

Collective-action situations, broadly defined, pervade both the public and private sectors of all countries. Collective-action *situations* become collective-action *problems* when actors in the situation choose actions that produce outcomes that are evaluated to be less desirable than others available to them. The classic example of a collective-action problem in the public sector is the provision of a public good such as a national highway network or the reduction of environmental harms (such as smog at a local level or global warming at a global level) (Olson 1965). Analysts tend to focus on solving collective-action problems through the public sector. Yet, as Miller (1992) has clearly demonstrated, simply creating a public bureaucracy to tackle the provision of public goods or the protection of natural resources does not automatically solve the initial collective-action problem and may even foster additional problems.

If development agencies and governments seek sustainable solutions to problems, then they will have to focus on more than just altering the biophysical-material world or a community's attributes. For example, building a pipeline to provide potable water to a village does change the material world, but such a fix will soon face the collective action problem of maintaining the tap over time. In addition to the tap's construction, rules will need to be constructed and enforced. Few governments—especially the poorer ones who receive development assistance—have the resources to maintain by themselves the entire infrastructure they build (E. Ostrom et al. 1993). Without a change or creation of rules-in-use, the potable water solution will eventually disappear. The creation of such rules is a collective problem in itself, influenced by biophysical-material conditions and community attributes.

The core questions faced by the members of any team effort in the public or private sector are who should contribute what, when, and where? Who will coordinate their efforts? How will joint returns be distributed? Unless participants share clear and efficiency-enhancing rules and norms, some may shirk their responsibilities and free ride on the efforts of others or try to deflect joint returns primarily to themselves. Once participants hold back on their contributions to joint efforts or allocate considerable time to gaining more than their share of benefits, the level of productive outcomes achieved by their joint efforts starts to deteriorate. Unfortunately, such dynamic processes lead toward lower and lower levels of returns for all involved, and the perverse incentives tend to be self-reinforcing. Thus, problems get worse and it is even more difficult to reverse the process.

In the 1960s and 1970s, the theoretical presumption was that citizens themselves could not solve most collective-action problems that involved public goods or common-pool resources, and that a centralized government was necessary to impose solutions (Olson 1965; Hardin 1968). Now, in light of considerable theoretical and empirical research, most institutional analysts recognize that individuals are capable of crafting solutions to their own diverse problems of collective action. Such solutions usually require a rich set of general and special institutional arrangements at local, regional, and national levels in both the private as well as public spheres of life (Scott 1998; V. Ostrom et al. 1988; McGinnis 1999*a* and *b*; V. Ostrom 1999; de Soto 2000; Dietz, et al. 2003). And different sectors will likely demand different institutional arrangements: the effective provision of national defense, for example, will not look like those that facilitate the protection of natural resources, the construction and maintenance of effective physical infrastructure, the provision of education, or the stimulation of technological innovation.

Successful institutional arrangements reflect, moreover, the nature of the collective-action problem that they are meant to solve. Following the IAD framework, we now look at a variety of generic collective action problems at the *operational level*. The collective action literature identifies several types of motivation problems under concepts such as common-pool resource problems, public goods problems, and asymmetric power. We then focus on how missing or asymmetric information about the actions or characteristics of individuals may also inhibit their fruitful cooperation. Here, researchers have identified several situations of information constraint, including principal–agent problems, moral hazard problems, and signaling problems.

Motivation Problems and Aid Failure

Core dysfunctional problems, present in all societies, tend to exist at an even greater extent in poor, aid-receiving countries. Assessing the aid effectiveness puzzle, we focus first on problems stemming primarily from an individual's inadequate motivation to contribute to the production of joint benefits even when the actor has complete information. These problems include public goods and common-pool resources. Motivation problems may also arise when power is asymmetrically distributed between actors. The elites in a society, for example, may resist more efficient arrangements that threaten their privileged status. Aid is likely to be ineffective when these problems of motivation remain unresolved.

The Public Goods Problem

Public goods (and services) are those that are consumed jointly by individuals, and which is difficult to exclude consumption by non-contributors, and where one person's consumption does *not* subtract from the availability of the good to others. In a basic public goods problem, a set of actors, who are all in similar positions, must decide whether or not to take costly actions that generate a net loss for each individual but produce a net benefit for the actors as a group. When the individual costs of providing a public good are less than the individual benefits derived from it (even though when many contribute they are all better off) standard theory holds that public goods will be underproduced. Mancur Olson has argued that "unless the number of individuals is quite small, or unless there is coercion or some other device to make individuals act in their common interest, *rational self-interested individuals will not act to achieve their common or group interests*" (1965: 2, emphasis in original). Not contributing to a joint effort when others do is "free-riding," as the non-contributor benefits. Of course, if no one contributes, there is no benefit on which to free ride.[7]

In many contemporary settings, individuals have created a wide diversity of institutional arrangements that allow them to provide local public goods through various forms of organization, from voluntary associations, to informal arrangements that closely approximate those found in the official public sector, to governments. For large-scale public goods—such as national defense—national governments are the prime mechanism used to provide (and produce) these public goods. Mixed public and private systems exist for the provision of many goods, such as public radio, where government subsidies supplement voluntary contributions made by citizens. Where communities create local public goods, one usually finds some complex of government and private organizations that have evolved or been self-consciously designed to overcome the perverse incentives that would otherwise lead to the underproduction of the public good.[8]

Aid donors frequently fund projects that provide public goods, such as school construction, that do not come about through local efforts due to a prevailing public good problem. While a donor may be able to finance the short-term provision of public goods in such instances, donor efforts often fail to address the underlying incentive problem, thus failing to generate a sustainable solution. Schools, for instance, require maintenance and repair. While each member of a village would like their school to be in good working order, each member also has the incentive to let another villager, or another infusion from a donor, take care of this need. Thus, the donor would have solved one collective-action problem by providing the school, but would also have created others that can lead to poor outcomes over time.[9]

Common-Pool Resources

Similar to public goods, excluding potential beneficiaries from the use of common-pool resources is difficult. Unlike public goods, however, one person's use does subtract from the resources available to others. Thus, in the absence of effective institutions, users will over-harvest common-pool resources; natural resources such as forests, fisheries, and grazing areas may even be destroyed.

Garrett Hardin (1968) paints a grim picture to characterize the "tragedy of the commons," thought by many to occur whenever multiple actors jointly use a single common-pool resource. Hardin's metaphor so dramatically captured the imagination of scholars, activists, and officials that major policies related to natural resources have been based on the presumed helplessness of the users themselves to change the structure of incentives they faced. For example, a 1980s Social Forestry Project funded by Sweden's aid agency in Orissa, India, assumed that a growing population of forest users was contributing to severe forest degradation. Funding from Sweden supported afforestation activities led by the Orissa Forest Department, which included tree planting and organizing cooperatively managed plantations to produce fuel wood. Little thought was given at the time, however, to helping the forest users revive their own indigenous rules and capacity for self-organization to promote sustainable forest use (Gibson et al. 2005: chapter 9).[10]

People may also create common-pool resources such as the treasuries of a national government or a private firm; similar tragedies of the commons can occur in these resources too. Increased pressure on a public treasury can lead to irresponsible budgetary behavior. The "harvesters" in this case are bureaucrats, local and national politicians, and interest groups who keep taking from a recurrent budget by calling for increased spending for their particular issue. The government budget is a common-pool resource since they can consume parts of the treasury at little cost to themselves (Campos and Pradhan 1996). Donor largesse, can, in some cases, create a fiscal commons that is ongoing and subject to few constraints and therefore are likely to produce inefficient and inequitable outcomes (see Eriksson Skoog 1998).

Theoretical and empirical findings, however, demonstrate that Hardin's predicted outcome does not hold in many cases. A large literature has identified many common-pool resource situations in which users of the resource have developed effective rules for governing and managing it over time (McCay and Acheson 1987; E. Ostrom 1990; Bromley et al. 1992). Institutions that limit harvesting exist in situations from rural watersheds to national budgets. Of course, the particulars of any specific harvesting situation differ dramatically from one location to another. Such research makes it important for donors to determine what the nature of the good is and, if it is a common-pool resource, not automatically disregard local level institutions that may be operating effectively already, or that might even be usefully revived and renewed.

Asymmetric Power

Persons facing public good and common-pool resource problems frequently also confront other actors with greater command over key resources. Such unequal distribution can have serious effects on the ability of governments or citizens to solve collective-action problems. Ostrom and Gardner (1993) provide the example of farmers located at the head end of an irrigation system, who have considerably more power to affect what happens downstream than the farmers located at the tail end. Empirical studies of irrigation systems in Nepal find that when the head-enders use a farmer-constructed irrigation system that does not need much maintenance, they tend to take most of the water and leave only what they cannot use for tailenders. In these cases, tailenders invest little effort in maintaining the system.

On the other hand, most farmer-constructed irrigation systems do require substantial maintenance. When the farmers themselves have created rules about how maintenance is to be supplied, tail-end farmers have considerably more bargaining power. They often demand, and obtain, a fair share of irrigation water in return for their contribution to the maintenance of the system (see Lam 1998). These systems also tend to produce the higher agricultural yields. When donors invest in irrigation systems without an understanding of these dynamics, they may reduce the bargaining power of the tailenders leading to lower levels of production and greater distributional problems (E. Ostrom 1996).

Many other sources of asymmetric power exist besides sheer location. Most collective-action problems occur within the context of a preexisting distribution of economic and political power. If that distribution is highly unequal, economic or political elites have likely ensured that past decisions distribute assets disproportionately to themselves. Solutions to collective-action problems can produce low productivity, but still generate enough advantage for those with asymmetric power to remain in place. If changes increase the joint outcomes for all, but leave the elite with less, they may resist the change.[11]

The solution to some collective-action problems may require the leadership and example of entrepreneurs who are willing to take initiative and invest more than an equal share of the effort needed to make the collective process work (Kuhnert 2001). When some individuals within a group have a disproportionate and larger stake in the solution of a particular collective dilemma, these individuals may be prepared to facilitate the solution of the problem. Although everyone will be better-off if the problem is solved, everyone but the entrepreneur will have an incentive to free ride on the efforts of others. The entrepreneur, on the other hand, will be motivated to monitor the compliance of the group members. Although the presence of an entrepreneur may provide a solution to the motivation problem inherent in many collective dilemmas, it does not provide a solution for all of them. For instance, as the entrepreneur tries to monitor the behavior of other group members, information asymmetries often complicate the effectiveness of such efforts.

Working for economic and social equality and environmental improvement requires finding peaceful means of productively and equitably combining the efforts (and often the unevenly distributed social and economic assets) of individuals. The individuals who are currently most powerful in recipient countries nearly always have the most to lose from changes leading to democratic development. They may forcibly resist such efforts. Achieving economic and political independence and democratic development requires substantial time and energy to be invested by a large number of individuals. Reducing poverty requires investing resources and hard work to create opportunities for the less advantaged.

Information Problems and Aid Failure

Development aid is also plagued by situations of incomplete information. Missing information refers to the knowledge that individuals have of their own time and place and that cannot be captured as data. Asymmetric information about actions characterizes a series of problems referred to as *moral hazard*.

Originally analyzed with regard to insurance problems, moral hazard problems are found whenever an actor is protected against risk partly resulting from that actor's own behavior. Another common situation characterized by asymmetric information is the *principal–agent* problem, which can be found whenever individuals work within a hierarchy. In the absence of countervailing institutions, these and other information related problems can preclude successful collective action.

Missing Information and Local Knowledge

Solving most public good and common-pool resource problems at the operational level requires considerable local knowledge. Friedrich Hayek (1948) recognized a body of important but unorganized knowledge that individuals, each in their particular circumstance, possess about their own time and place. This knowledge by its nature cannot be tabulated, and thus is difficult to use systematically. Such specific time and place knowledge also contrasts with objective scientific knowledge, which emphasizes the placement of observed regularities within some theoretical context. Hayek (1952b) stressed that given the issue of time-and-place knowledge, methods of scientific analysis appropriate for physical phenomena cannot be applied uniformly without qualification to understand the social-economic nexus.[12]

Often individuals acting within a particular situation over a long period hold the most pertinent knowledge. For example, farmers who have used a stream to irrigate crops are usually well aware of where the stream crosses solid rock as contrasted to where the stream crosses a long section of sandy and unstable soil. If the engineers designing a donor-funded irrigation project do not learn this information, the canal may wash out after only a few years of operation, as Hilton (2002) graphically describes in an analysis of some donor-funded projects in Nepal.

A central challenge in aid lies in incorporating both time-and-place knowledge and scientific knowledge as they exist in the many contexts of development. While increasing project costs in the short run, drawing on both knowledge types is likely to enhance sustainability and thus efficiency over the longer term. In this regard, designs that allow beneficiaries joint ownership over a project or program would likely be able to integrate local knowledge more easily.

Moral Hazard Problems

Moral hazard problems exist in a wide variety of settings where individuals contract to indemnify themselves against loss regardless of their efforts to avoid such loss. The concept originates from the difficulties of insurance companies to create effective insurance institutions. At least some individuals will be more careless after obtaining insurance, and insurance companies cannot afford to monitor each individual's behavior at all times. Since observing actions is costly, and since the individual is now protected from loss, the protection itself may reduce the likelihood that the actor takes preventive measures.

More broadly, the term *moral hazard* is used to refer to problems of hidden action (Campbell 1995). Moral hazard problems can lead to aid failures, for example, when government officials are "insured" from poor performance through their patronage of high officials or even through civil service labor protection rules.

Another example of moral hazard occurs when recipient governments promise to take costly future actions to reform political or economic institutions in exchange for immediate financial support from a donor. The aid itself, however, can encourage the recipients to delay these reforms even longer than they would have in the absence of aid (Eriksson Skoog 1998; van de Walle 2000; Gibson and Hoffman 2005). "The indiscriminate availability of aid creates a moral hazard, where aid availability, by 'insuring' incompetent governments from the results of their actions, allows governments to postpone reform efforts and weakens their incentive to find alternative revenue sources" (Bräutigam 2000: 24).

Principal–Agent Situations

Much of productive life is organized in hierarchies in which individuals in decision situations are arrayed in a series of superior-subordinate positions. In the idealized hierarchy, a superior defines what, how, when, and where a subordinate works. He or she also evaluates the subordinate in light of these instructions. Implicitly, this model assumes that the superior is aware of the actions of the subordinate and can thus reward performance. Until recently, this simple model was part of most recommendations made by donors to developing countries to generate better policy outcomes (V. Ostrom 1988; Wunsch 2000).

Work in the political economy tradition has found this simple model of hierarchy—and thus bureaucracy—fundamentally flawed. Numerous scholars have shown that such institutions are riddled with problems of asymmetric information, generated by their inherent principal–agent relationships (Alchian and Demsetz 1972; Tirole 1986). In a principal–agent relationship, the principal is the individual (or the representative for an organized set of individuals) who benefits from the outcomes achieved by the agent, while the agent is offered a contract to take the appropriate actions to achieve these outcomes. A problem occurs in this relationship since the agent may have different preferences than his or her principal, and the principal has only coarse information about the agent's actions (Rasmusen 1989).

The common example of an isolated principal–agent situation occurs when an individual consults a doctor or a lawyer. As the principal, the individual asks an agent for professional services to increase the principal's welfare. The individual, however, does not have a guarantee that the professional will thoroughly consider their interest and provide them the best service. One of the mechanisms used around the world to reduce the difficulties in principal–agent problems is to create professional associations that monitor the performance of their own members. It is in the interest of the professionals to be able to claim higher reliability in serving the interest of their clients by adopting a professional code and being a member of a professional association. The ability to bring lawsuits for malpractice is another mechanism available to principals who believe they were not well served.

In larger organizations, hierarchies contain a series of principal–agent relationships, breeding both an incentive problem and an ever-increasing problem of missing information and asymmetric information. At each level there is a reduction in the level of information passed along to superiors; the larger the chain of staff, the smaller will be the proportion of the information known to those at the bottom that reaches the top (Williamson 1967, 1973). This reduction of information becomes magnified by the subordinates' incentive to pass information favorable to their own performance. Those at the top of the chain consequently receive limited and biased information.

Organizations have designed a variety of institutions to mitigate these problems. Private firms attempt to tie work and pay tightly together through such arrangements as piecework contracts, commissions, and bonuses, or stock options for firm profitability (Milgrom and Roberts 1992). Entry-level staff members in organizations may be motivated to work hard by the promise of promotions to positions with more responsibility, status, and pay based on performance. But given the complexity of work assignments, no complete contract can be written covering all exigencies and specifying what will happen to the agent under each circumstance, even in the private sector (Grossman and Hart 1986).

Solving the problems resulting from asymmetric information in public bureaucracies is much more difficult than in private sector firms. Governments charge public agencies with a variety of objectives that are difficult to measure, making equally difficult the evaluation about an agency's efforts (let alone any one staff member's contribution to outcomes) (Tirole 1994). The kind of contracts offered to employees of government agencies is also much more limited. In developing countries, the pay of public employees is frequently much less than the competitive wage; such low wages are often offset by a promise of a relatively long-term contract. Civil service regulations often create barriers to firing a government worker for lack of performance. While citizen organizations are able to monitor some aspects of the work of street-level public servants, the work of most public employees is carried out far from public view. And although schools of public administration stress the professional nature of public service, no professional association has taken on as strong and active a role regarding public officials as have associations of medical doctors and lawyers.

The combination of low pay and long-term employment also exacerbates the severity of moral hazard problems faced in public bureaucracies, particularly in developing countries. Public employees may devote their working time to a wide diversity of private activities such as running their own private businesses. Instead of just the shirking associated with principal–agent relationships, public employees may need to find ways of gaining private returns to make their investment in obtaining a public position worthwhile, such as extracting side payments from citizens wishing to obtain a license or who are suspected of committing a crime.

Adverse Selection and Signaling

Actors' characteristics, in addition to their actions, can be private information. An adverse selection problem occurs when an individual has private knowledge that others do not share. For example, the individual may have private knowledge about an object that the individual would like to sell (Akerlof 1970) or about his or her own skills as a worker (Spence 1973).

Adverse selection problems occur whenever the selection of beneficiaries or future employees is a nonrandom process that tends to select the least-productive individuals. This logic helps explain why it is so difficult to devise a sustainable, private health insurance or unemployment insurance scheme. The problem facing health insurance or unemployment schemes is that those least likely to need the insurance are the most likely to opt out of the system. That makes the pool of individuals remaining in the insurance scheme even more likely to incur sickness or unemployment. The rates must then increase. This leads again to a dropout of the individuals who are least likely to draw on the insurance at the new price. Over time, the scheme's costs become ever higher, and those that remain ever more likely to draw on benefits.

This structure of incentives prevents private markets from solving adverse selection problems. Putting the insurance scheme in the public sector may solve the adverse selection problem by greatly expanding the pool of insured to include healthier, as well as less healthy individuals—but it may not solve the moral hazard problem!

Similar processes occur in development aid. As donor agencies ratchet up the conditions (analogous to the costs in the insurance example) to be met by recipients in exchange for aid, those in least need of aid (analogous to the healthy) will opt to leave the pool of possible recipients. This leaves those less able to meet the conditions in the pool, and seeing this, creates incentives for the aid agency to increase the conditions on receiving aid. Eventually, the riskiest projects will remain.

The private information that is held by individuals and leads to adverse selection problems may be discovered by others involved in an ongoing situation at some cost. Before hiring a new employee, for example, firms try to obtain relevant information about education, skills, and past work performance. Some of this may be acquired by testing; the rest by various screening processes. This information, however, is always an imperfect indicator of the quality of a future staff member. This is a particularly puzzling problem for agencies working in recipient countries that want to hire local staff members. How excellence is signaled in one culture may differ substantially from the signals that an individual would use in another culture. It is even a problem for how staff members within a development agency itself signal their skills to superiors.[13] If they are too overt in trying to show their skills, other staff members may resent their efforts. If they are too humble, they may be overlooked when a promotion opportunity occurs.

The Institutional Contexts of Aid

People all over the world confront operational situations of various types, such as those previewed above, where perverse incentives preclude them from realizing the gains from social cooperation. In developed countries, many of these potentially negative incentives are mitigated through institutions that, by restructuring situations of daily life, lead to mutually beneficial outcomes. In poor countries, by contrast, citizens often continue to face incentives that make it difficult to invest in economic activities, to provide public goods, to manage common-pool resources, and generally to arrive at mutually beneficial day-to-day arrangements.

Many scholars argue that development results from a broad set of institutional arrangements that facilitate a wide diversity of enforceable contractual arrangements (North 1990, 1994). When embedded in an open public realm with an effective property-rights system, and an available and fair court system, individuals can build trusting relationships that enable them to increase the benefits that they jointly obtain.

Arriving at these institutional arrangements requires that we understand the nature of numerous collective-action situations that pervade the social context. Many of these are repetitive situations that are poorly resolved in countries receiving large quantities of development assistance. To be effective and sustainable, a donor's intervention has to help solve underlying collective-action problems—not just provide the temporary infusion of funds and jobs associated with a project. This response, in turn, should incorporate the local knowledge about the needs, preferences, and problems of target beneficiaries that only they themselves possess. Access to this localized knowledge requires active beneficiary ownership rather than just the consumption of whatever is produced or distributed.

Aid and Indigenous Institutional Capital

Such local knowledge can often be found embedded in indigenous institutions, where the appropriateness of these institutional settings for development depends on the repertoire of design principles that individuals possess and on their experience in crafting rules to adapt to contemporary challenges. Indigenous institutions contain a wide variety of normative prescriptions that help constitute a basis for an adaptive community of understanding. Yet, while such institutions have enabled groups to solve collective-action problems in the past, they may not necessarily be applicable "as-is" to new situations or be legal in some contemporary settings. Further, they may have been perverted over time for partisan purposes, through negligence, or as a result of misunderstandings by external authorities, and thus produce poor outcomes.[14] These indigenous institutions, nevertheless, represent a reality that has to be accounted for.

In developing countries, aid projects and programs frequently address the manifestations or outcomes of institutional failures. The intervention by a foreign donor can introduce additional actors and rules to the action arena. These often reflect institutional understandings formed within the cultural context of the donor's own community. New rules and constraints are necessarily interpreted, however, by the developing country learner within the context of his or her own institutional context.

These contexts vary enormously as communities differ along numerous dimensions: population, assets, history, ethnicity, education, and the like. These factors affect individuals' capacity to self-organize, although the importance of any single attribute, or mix of attributes, will likely vary from context to context. For example, communities that have had a long history of solving their collective-action problems will likely have a better chance of doing so again when they confront another such problem. This community might be able to piggy back new solutions on existing institutions, might have a larger reservoir of trust upon which to draw, and it may have a longer time horizon than other communities without such a history (E. Ostrom 1990).

Unless external aid initiatives build on existing institutional understandings and hence "improve" them in terms of their ability to overcome particular collective-action problems, aid may hinder rather than promote development.

Without learning, any resolution to the underlying problem will be unsustainable. Indeed, ownership in aid takes meaning when the individuals confronting a collective-action problem are poised to modify an institutionalized system of incentives by drawing on past learning to change the structure of the incentives they face. Ominously, however, aid can erode or undermine local social capital when the rules and constraints that come along with it are placed carelessly in inappropriate interaction with other elements within the local structure of social capital (Morss 1984). When this happens, social capital is destroyed, learning is inhibited, and the developing society is left poorer for the aid it has received.

Missing, Weak, or Bad Institutions

In most countries receiving large amounts of development aid, institutions needed to cope adaptively with problems of collective action are either missing, weak, or bad. In countries with missing public institutions, individuals must deal primarily with their own family and networks of friends and neighbors to solve some of these basic problems. Pockets of highly productive and ingenious solutions to some problems of collective action can emerge from such networks but these are usually limited in scope and time.

In countries with weak or bad institutions, there may be an extensive public sector with many formal laws about solving some of these problems of collective action. But rather than facilitate solutions, such public sector agencies may use their authority against those who are trying to create productive opportunities for themselves and others. For example, underpaid public servants may resort to obtaining additional funds from side-payments extracted from citizens who need official approval for some action; the more steps required to comply with formal laws, the more opportunities exist for citizens to become discouraged (and for public officials to extract side-payments). In a sobering example of this problem, de Soto (2000) documents the 728 different bureaucratic steps required by the City of Lima for a resident to obtain a legal title to a home.[15]

When a public authority creates and enforces rules, individuals have an incentive to propose rules that give them advantages over others. Profits greater than those that would be available from an open, competitive process are referred to as *rents*; the process of seeking rules to give these advantages is *rent-seeking* behavior. Successful rent-seeking strategies may lead to very substantial costs imposed on others. Those who have been successful in the past in obtaining privileges may then become entrenched in a patron–client system whereby the elite keep themselves in an advantaged system by distributing rents to their clients in return for their support.

Improving the Institutional Context for Aid

Aid has not been effective in many contexts because it has not been sufficiently grounded in the institutional roots of development. Achieving broader development goals requires that we craft institutions that solve problems of collective action at various levels of social organization.

Changing the rules used at an *operational level* may improve joint outcomes substantially. Reaching an agreement on an appropriate change in rules and then monitoring and enforcing those rules in an efficient, fair, and open manner is, however, an extremely challenging task. It may require defining new positions of authority and ensuring that actors in these new positions face appropriate incentives and have sufficient information to act in a manner more consistent with reaching the goals spelled out in public policy.

The *collective choice level* is where individuals create rules that govern operational level behaviour. Both a village council and a government ministry are examples of collective choice level arenas. Here, individuals can potentially create new rules to solve operational-level collective-action problems through informal face-to-face discussions. However, making these changes sustainable over time can be difficult. Addressing problems of collective action at collective choice level confronts obstacles both similar and different to those reviewed at the operational level. Like the operational level, motivational and information problems haunt the efforts of policymaking bodies. The next chapter discusses how policymaking within the organization of a state can fail to provide the institutional basis for development.

The distribution of authority to engage in collective-choice arenas results from an amalgam of decisions made at the *constitutional choice level* where individuals produce rules about who participates over which decisions at the collective choice level. Changing the rules (institutions) at the policymaking level may improve joint outcomes substantially, but perverse incentive structures at this level can throw up sizeable barriers to solving the collective-action problems of development. Such perverse incentives in the collective-choice arena can make it difficult to create policies (collective choices) that can solve these problems rather than making them worse. Here, we again find basic problems related to motivation and information. Informational problems may be especially difficult given the uncertainties associated with major institutional changes. Parts II and III of this book attempt to reconcile the development puzzle from this *constitutional level* of analysis.

CHAPTER 4

The State as a Concept in Development

C haracteristics associated with advanced human development and rapid economic growth arise through the forms of productive association that human beings refer to (whether consciously or tacitly) in their actions and interactions with each other. How well individuals come together to solve problems—and in this way realize their innovative potential—depends on the nature of evolved as well as deliberately constituted institutions through which they associate.

Given the emphasis in postwar theories of development on a particular model of the state, what institutional role does this state play in promoting forms of productive association? And, what traps arise from this conceptual system? This chapter argues that the prevailing postwar concept of the state leads to intellectual dilemmas with negative consequences for development.

The Implicit Model of the State

Much of the modern development literature relies (if implicitly) on a model of state governance comparable to that conceived by Thomas Hobbes (1960).[1] Hobbes' state, a social-scientific abstraction, is constituted metaphorically of a sovereign head (or rulership) and of a body and limbs (or administration.) In its modern context, the state is often idealized in terms of an effective rulership soliciting information about problems present within given territorial boundaries and formulating policies needed to resolve them. An administration then carries out the policy assignments needed to promote the collective security and welfare of the state's subjects.

The Rulership

Thomas Hobbes justified sovereign rulership by identifying a need for a unity of power and law to maintain peace and order in the commonwealth. In a situation where individuals are not constrained by a system of public rules, noted Hobbes, each is free to take what he wills. At the same time, each has to defend what he has got against acquisition by others. In such situation, there is potential for conflict, diminishing the prospect for each to advance his well-being; life in these circumstances, as he famously put it, would be "solitary, poor, nasty, brutish, and short." (Ibid.)

Hobbes argued for a unity of power to maintain the unity of law critical for harmony in social relations, where this unity is manifested in a monopoly over the prerogatives of governance.[2] These include the powers to coerce others as necessary to enforce the rule of law and to secure the collective defense.[3]

Much of postwar development literature relies, if often implicitly, on a system of unified governance, where the state possesses monopoly prerogatives over collective problem-solving and conflict resolution—if at least as the ultimate arbitrator.[4] The need for specialization in problem-solving—based on superior access to information and experience in policymaking—underlies this prerogative. This singular source of law making authority, administrative organization, and coercive force is seen to further ensure social unity and organizational coherence. The state, in the postwar framework, emerges as such a problem-solving entity. Development economics, in this tradition, relies on the state as the principal instrument for alleviating poverty, encouraging equity, and directing economic growth and human development.[5] Here, society—whether centralized or decentralized—is organized with reference to a single center of authority.[6]

The Administration

In order to forge a unity among its subjects, to produce public goods, and to attend to the common defense, the rulership of a state must first gather information on conditions considered problematic, analyze this data, and develop appropriate policy recommendations.[7] The ruler then chooses among the recommendations and refers his decision to a bureaucratic organization for execution. Successful governance is achieved when statistical data is more complete, policy analysis is more thorough, policy choice is more principled, and policy implementation is more meticulous.

Sabetti's (2002) account of the unification and statehood of Italy, describes this model of the state:

> The new nation-state was organized as a single centre of authority with an exclusive monopoly on the use of physical force in the organization of society. The monopoly

over the supply of public goods and services was accomplished by a single overarching system of public administration with locally elected officials and professionally trained personnel hierarchically ordered and subject to direction by heads of departments at the centre of government. The creators of the Italian state anticipated that forced creation of unity through administrative measures under a common parliament, backed by a national army, would produce both good policies and good individuals by (1) forging the diverse communities of peoples into one strong and self-governing nation, (2) insuring a uniform provision of public services, and (3) removing once and for all the spectre of foreign intervention in Italian affairs.

This unity through centralized policy and administration is a hallmark of the postwar development paradigm (Hicks 1961). As such, the potential for development rests on the effectiveness of the ruler, and the effectiveness of the ruler depends, in turn, on how well this policy process operates.[8] A failure to develop is thus commonly identified with poor policy advice and with shortcomings in administration.

Is the concept of the state a viable proposition? Scholars in the Austrian and Public Choice traditions in economics have long pointed out that problems related to knowledge and self-interest motivations pose fundamental impediments to the state's ability to foster development through policy development, policy choice, and policy administration. These well-known views challenge the *competence* of the state. Following a quick overview of these arguments we will see why the *concept* of the state itself fails to provide a robust foundation for development.

Challenging the Competence of the State

A particular notion of the state, core to the postwar view of development, raises two specific considerations.[9] The *Knowledge Problem* points out that full knowledge of time and space contingencies contained in society cannot be gained by agents of a state, no matter how enlightened or well-informed (Hayek 1945). *Government Failure* points out that self-interest motivations apply to those empowered to select and administer policy, as it does to all others (Buchanan and Tullock 1962). These core notions challenge the competence of the state.

Knowledge Asymmetries: Data versus Knowledge

The standard development literature consistently links effective policy development with the possession of detailed knowledge of what is going on society. The ability of a state to solve problems encountered by its subjects relies on adequate information on which to develop appropriate policy responses and with which to sensitize policymakers to take the appropriate actions.

An example of this approach is be seen in recent efforts assumed by the United Nations to collect data on the value of nonmarket work as an input to national policymaking.[10] Following the Fourth World Conference on Women, held in Beijing in 1995, the United Nations was directed to develop standards by which statistical agencies of member nations are to develop aggregate measures "to recognize and make visible the full extent of the work of women and all their contributions to the national economy including their contributions to the unremunerated and domestic sectors, and [to] examine the relationship of women's unremunerated work to their incidence of their vulnerability to poverty."[11] The reasoning for this directive, set out in the Platform for Action adopted in Beijing, was that unless adequate data was available, appropriate policies could not be developed to deal with the poverty, discrimination, and disenfranchisement faced by many women in the developing world.[12]

The Beijing platform identifies a key problem—and, indeed, the failure of adopted policy to identify and cure perceived problems *is* rooted in inadequate knowledge. Policies have been conducted in ignorance of its effects on poor women and other groups, and have contributed to conditions of extreme personal hardship (see for example, McGow 1995). However, the simple matter is that the sort of knowledge that is required for the policy-based centralized problem-solving cannot be collected. Statistical agencies if given a sufficient budget can collect voluminous data on observable conditions. However, knowledge that each of us possess in our understanding of each other and our particular problem environment can never be sufficiently captured as an input to policy (Lavoie 1985).

The *Knowledge Problem*, in short, is the contention that a centralized problem-solver, even if benevolent and well-meaning, lacks the knowledge to combine the resources available in society in a meaningful manner. As Hayek (1945) points out in *The Use of Knowledge in Society*,

> The peculiar character of the problem of a rational economic order is determined precisely by the fact that the knowledge of the circumstances of which we must make use never exists in concentrated or integrated form but solely as the dispersed bits of incomplete and frequently contradictory knowledge which all the separate individuals possess. The economic problem of society is thus not merely a problem of how to allocate "given" resources—if "given" is taken to mean given to a single mind that deliberately solves the problem set by the "data." It is rather a problem of how to secure the best use of resources known to any of the members of society, for ends whose relative importance only these individuals know. Alternatively, to put it briefly, it is a problem of the utilization of knowledge that is not given to anyone in its totality.

Hayek goes on to note that the main economic problem is one of individuals adapting rapidly to changes in their particular circumstance. In this, we are each more aware about the exigencies of our own "time and place." We interpret this information with respect to a sensory order that we have developed over the course of our biological and psychological, cultural, and linguistic development as concerns the problems that we encounter and have had experience in assessing and solving.

Although the idea of the state as a problem-solving device relies on the collection of data as the knowledge base for considered policy action, such data cannot extract the knowledge that each individual in society has of his or her own physical and temporal circumstance. Therefore, this calls into doubt the epistemic competence of the state.

Motivation Problems: Enlightenment versus Self-Interest

In the standard model of the state, policy is formulated by experts and adopted by enlightened agents of government. Yet, policy advice as developed by economists and other experts relies on relatively simplified perspectives of complex social and economic realities.[13] Since a multiplicity of such worldviews can be developed, there are in turn many models as well as many associated recommendations as to what might be done to solve some perceived problem. There is as well a diversity of interests among those to whom such advice is proffered. Given the diversity of choices, what governs the selection of policy advice?[14] Below are two alternative scenarios.

In the idealized policy arena, enlightened policymakers, selflessly dedicated to improving the public's welfare, solicit advice from policy analysts as to how best serve their interests. On one side of the exchange are economists who dedicate themselves to the scientific pursuit of objective knowledge about the workings of the economy. Based on such assessments, they reach conclusions as to what should be done. In the idealized policy arena, differences of opinion among policymakers as to the best course for improving public welfare are resolved by recourse to scientific consensus. This consensus is approached through scientific competition, based on the soundness of the assumptions used in the theoretical framework, the logical derivations based on these, on the robustness of data gathered and used, and on the consistent interpretation of the resulting policy implications. This view of the *market for policy* employs assumptions not only about the behavior of the players but also of the epistemological foundations of economics and the role of government in diagnosing and correcting the problems faced by society.

Consider, in contrast to the idealized view of the market for policy, a Public Choice view. Following upon the skepticism expressed by Adam Smith as to the benevolence of the butcher, the brewer, or the baker, economists are accustomed to characterizing businessmen as acting to serve in their own interests. Yet, policymakers and their economist advisors, no less than the rest of the populace, are interested in their own personal welfare (Buchanan and Tullock 1962; Brennan and Buchanan 1985).

In browsing the policy bazaar, policymakers can select, from among the diversity of theoretical opinion and policy conclusions, those interpretations that lend legitimacy to particular decisions thought to further political goals. A greater selection among such advice has become available over the past several decades with economists among the most pervasive and influential among such policy entrepreneurs. In this regard, Niskanen (1986: 236) notes that while the plethora of policy advice available today may partly be attributable to the increased role of government over the same period, the "broader role of the economist as policy advisor may be found in the usefulness of economic skills in providing types of information valued by the politician." Niskanen (1986: 243) goes on to note that "for the most part, politicians employ policy advisors who serve their interests" particularly when opinion among economists is divided over a policy issue.

In contrast to the idealized market for policy advice, in the real world, self-seeking and opportunistic players select from among a multiplicity of policy alternatives.[15] Buchanan and Wagner (1977) point out that Keynes' assumptions—that fiscal policy will be developed by a select cadre of "Harvey Road" economists and promoted by a ruling elite—is defective in this respect. The consequences of Keynesian fiscal policy, observe Buchanan and Wagner, vary when such models include assumptions that elected politicians respond to pressure from their constituents, special interest lobbies, and from the bureaucracy.

If we accept that those vested with the authority to find solutions to problems afflicting members of the public may act on motives associated with their own self-interest rather than enlightened public interest, then the very competence of the State as a problem-solver is put in doubt.

Administering Public Policy: Weberian Ideal versus Reality

Beyond the tasks of gathering the relevant knowledge, developing the necessary policy recommendations, and adopting them, lies the issue of policy implementation. Here too, we can question the competence of the state as a problem-solver.

In the Wilsonian and Weberian traditions development administration, *Politics*—which is taken to be concerned with the formulation and legislation of public policy—is taken to be distinct from *Public Administration*—which is seen as a systematic execution of these policies as expressed in legislation (Heady 2001). A professional civil service is envisaged that can efficiently transform policy into reality. The Weberian bureaucracy, as an ideal type, is a well-oiled machine of interchangeable parts, immune from politics, which is designed to mobilize resources to realize policy aims. It is an objective organization of conduct operating according to calculable rules. The professionalism of the bureaucrat constrains his or her actions.

In the real world, however, the behavior of officials is also conditioned by reigning institutions. Here, bureaucratic behavior can develop at variance with the Weberian or Wilsonian ideal. Robert Wade's (1985) study of an irrigation bureaucracy in a state in southern India is illustrative in this regard.

Highlighting the rules within a centralized bureaucratic system in South India, where job transfers serve as rewards and disciplinary devices, Wade, describes "a special circuit of transactions in which the bureaucracy acquires funds, partly from clients and partly from the state treasury, channels these funds up to the higher ranks and politicians, the latter in turn using the funds for distributing short term inducements in exchange for electoral support" (Ibid.). Wade's observations reveal that poorly designed and insufficiently conditioned structures of bureaucratic governance are susceptible to undesirable patterns of behavior. As an example of a pervasive phenomenon, it calls to question the competence of centralized systems of public administration as a generic component of state governance.

Indeed, the competence of bureaucrats is also constrained by the limited "time and place" information they posses. At the same time, they may have access to certain types of privileged information that they can use to their own advantage, raising again the problems of motivation discussed earlier.

The Intellectual Crisis of State Governance

The state, as abstractly constituted in postwar development theory, represents one organizational context for ordering relationships among individuals. It promises coherence to those who choose to think in general about issues of social order and development by consolidating problem-solving through centralized policy management rather than emphasize the need for institutions as nodal points for locally based decision making. This logic of a centrally integrated problem-solving device is vulnerable to information asymmetries because it cannot capture the knowledge of time and place. Policy prescriptions based on its abstract underpinnings do not necessarily motivate sufficient problem-solving effort by humans where problems of cooperation and coordination related to the particulars of time and place can arise.

The idea of the "state" taken up in the postwar framework of development—by offering the possibility of elegant theoretical solutions to complex problems of collective action found in each of many cultural and geographic settings—thus presents a chimera that leads away from the difficult task of addressing the problems of association within specific problem arenas.

Abstract interpretations of the state can lead, moreover, to modes of problem-solving characterized by ideological debates. Ideologies—often masked in the rhetorical formalisms of economics—appear to offer deceptively simple, broad, credible, and scientifically grounded solutions to very complex problems.

In this, ideologies distract from the need for individuals to engage with others in their community to overcome shared problems.

The theoretical convenience of the state, on which much development analysis is based, also leads us away from a more basic appreciation of the role of democratic processes within systems of collective action. Policy efforts aimed as advice to a sovereign can draw attention away from core problem-solving efforts among citizens. As we see below, these factors, together, contribute to an "intellectual crisis" in development administration (V. Ostrom 1973).

The Great Antimony: Between High Theory and Complex Reality

Humans impose their finite minds upon a complex reality. We cope with the complexity around us by categorizing encountered objects and effects in some manner considered relevant and then by relating them through the use of concepts (Newell and Simon 1972). While the world presents a buzzing, blooming confusion, we make use of provisional bounds with which to make sense of our surroundings.[16] In this respect, growth of knowledge can be thought of in terms of both revising and developing new categories and concepts as well as exploiting existing ones to solve problems as they are perceived.

As such, problem-solving has its inductive and deductive components. As W. Brian Arthur (1994) notes,

> In problems of complication then, we look for patterns; and we simplify the problem by using these to construct temporary internal models or hypotheses or *schemata* to work with. We carry our localized deductions based on our current hypotheses and act on them. As feedback from the environment come in, we may strengthen or weaken our beliefs in our current hypotheses, discarding some when they cease to perform, and replacing them as needed with new ones.

In regarding our complex economic and social environment, we similarly rely on certain theoretical schemata or perspective to render it intelligible. Since any perspective of the nature of social structures is subjective, there is arguably no "right way" of looking at things. Still, the view from particular theoretical vantages, and the deductive inferences we may draw from them, may be more useful than others are in framing conjectured solutions to problems of cooperation and social order.

One way of arranging our perceptions is to make a clear distinction between positive and normative analysis. The view of the New Chicago School, prominent in economics, holds that positive science should be driven toward generating useful implications and predictions *regardless of the level of realism* in the generating assumptions. As Milton Friedman (1953) famously noted, "the ultimate goal of a positive science is the development of a theory or hypothesis that yields valid and meaningful predictions about phenomena not yet observed."

This positivist approach is indicative of a pronounced inclination among many postwar economists to discern a general theory, a *science* of society founded on conceptual artifices, that governs all economic and social behavior. As G.L.S. Shackle (1967) notes, "in the description of the world, a universal, all-pervasive uniformity, simplicity, and unity is assuredly the aim of science, and various sciences at various times appear to take long strides towards its attainment." The development of *high theory* in economics, in order to provide a generalized explanation for viewed regularities in economic and social behavior, follows this aim. The use of these principles is regarded as enabling the scientific control of such behavior to the benefit of mankind. As such, economists have made significant intellectual investments in the imagined concepts of *homo œconomicus* and of *equilibrium* as bases on which to build this high theory.[17]

This general theoretic approach in economics is defended on the grounds that the alternative—that is to understand economic life with all its interrelations in its full reality—is simply not possible. At the same time, however, abstracted theories that strive for a universal, all-pervasive simplicity contribute little understanding to how individuals cope in practical terms with the problem situations of their environs. Hayek (1937: 35) observed in his essay *Economics and Knowledge* that while economic theory is marked by an "excessive preoccupation" with such abstractions, these can be severely misleading when extrapolated, as they routinely are, beyond their narrow analytical frame of validity.[18]

A gulf—what Walter Eucken (1992) referred to as "The Great Antimony"—thus appears between that which seems to be theoretically possible but effectively meaningless in practical problem-solving, and that which is appropriate but seemingly not theoretically tractable. Noting that "to understand economic reality is to understand all of this economic activity in its entirety, and how it fits together," Eucken distinguishes between the *general theoretical aspect*, which requires "reasoning, analysis, and an elaboration of analytical models" and the *historical aspect* of the economic problem, which calls for "perception, intuition, synthesis, understanding, and a feeling for living individual experience" (Ibid.).

The dilemma faced by the United Nations to follow-up on the mandate of the Fourth World Conference on Women exemplifies Eucken's Great Antimony. National Income accounting, based on economic "high" theory developed by Hicks, Debreau, and others, uses price as a proxy for value in gauging GNP.[19] This leaves national accountants at a disadvantage to develop a robust measure of the value of goods and services that are not mediated in formal markets and that do not bear an explicit price. At the same time historical approaches, as highlighted, appeal to our perceptions, intuitions, and understandings about the value of work performed (often by women) in informal market settings (Shivakumar 2000). Some advocates have argued that unless policymakers have access to statistics that quantify the contributions individuals make outside the formal economy, their interests will continue to be neglected by policymakers.[20] The example, here, reveals that high theory can defy reconciliation with complex reality.

A proper consideration of the potential for human well-being, in this and other respects, remains stymied in how we continue to choose to theorize about the complex world we inhabit. A framework for development, based on the state and the abstract theoretical apparatus for policy that conforms to it, poses fundamental puzzles that challenge the often accepted framework of state governance.

Ideology, Deception, and the State

When analysts offer policy remedies to a ruler, they in effect refer to a hypothesized solution to a given problem (Dewey 1982). As hypotheses, such policies are to be evaluated on the consequences that ensue from their adoption. What, however, is the basis for this evaluation: Are policies to be judged by their consequences to the public or to the policymaker?

This issue takes on particular relevance when, as in the organization of a state, the rulership is set apart from the subjects. In such an instance, it is well possible that those who exercise the prerogative of rulership face a different reality or *raison d'état* than those who are subjects. Do we measure the success of a policy based on its ability to secure and maintain the ruler's hold on power or on its usefulness in solving problems faced by individuals in society? Ideology and deception go hand in hand. In this regard, Vincent Ostrom (1997: 55) notes that "the place of ideas in the discourse about public affairs may be subject to a selective bias in which glittering generalities, slogans, and sonorous phrases are used to appeal to voters." Ideologies, he notes, as abstract theories and aims that establish a political program, become cloaks for the strategic manipulation of the public; they are—in terms of an alternate metaphor—the tools of deception.[21] A framework for development that builds on the myth of the unitary state as a capable problem-solving device in all contexts is misleading.[22]

Relatedly, McCloskey (1997) notes that although economists claim to argue on the basis of statistical inference, positivism, and the use of sophisticated mathematical representations, what actually takes place are appeals to reason, precedent, and consistency, backed up by rough estimates and "ad hockery." The *rhetoric of economics*—the necessity of establishing credibility along these lines—has overtaken the need to continue a meaningful and fruitful dialogue. McCloskey states that the fear among many economists appears to be that their commentaries, observations, and advice would be questioned and be open to greater skepticism should their presentations be stripped of their pseudo-scientific appurtenances.

Further to this point, Mirowski (1992) notes that the use of the metaphor of classical physics in neoclassical economics creates the illusion that the state can solve problems affecting its subjects by controlling the hydraulic levers of fiscal and monetary policy.[23] This, he notes, is a form of deception that has progressed so far that this metaphor now controls the agenda in economics. Indeed, economists working the "mainstream" tradition increasingly have come to believe that the world of their policy models represents the ideal and that the real world consequently represents an aberration.

As such, it appears that there is little that cannot be classified as a failure in comparison to models that presume perfect information and no costs of transaction, and which cannot be posed therefore as a problem for the state to solve. This presents numerous opportunities for entrepreneurship in policy action where initiatives to the private advantage can be masked as responses to the concerns of the public. In this respect, the rhetorical flourish of economic high theory can become a tool for deception. It can be, in the absence of adequate constitutional constraints, a way for the rulership, as justified "scientifically," to pursue its self-interests as and when they may see them, while impressing their subjects of their concern for them and of their superior talents in problem-solving.

In this way, economics as a "general science of development" based on the ideology of the state as a centralized problem-solving device, is prone to be detached from its scientific purpose. It can instead become amenable to misuse as a rhetorical device for the rulership to pursue narrow objectives and self-interests. In this way, economics threatens, ironically, to become a part of the double-talk and deception that underlie the pathologies of underdevelopment.

The foundations of development economics—based on high theory as geared toward a theory of the state as a centralized problem-solving device—can foster a discourse on policy distant from the practical difficulties that individuals face in their various exigencies. It can lend the illusion that policymakers are capable of dealing with the problem-solving and conflict resolution even while far removed from the actualities faced by the individual on the spot.

When, by being lulled by ideological palliatives in our political discourse, we cease to employ our intellects to marshal and refashion real and institutional resources as to solve problems as relevant to each of us in our own time and place, we harm prospects for development. As Vincent Ostrom (1997: 131) concludes, "the deceptions inherent in gross oversimplifications may evoke self-deceptions. Those who fool others are likely to fool themselves and they may threaten the viability of human societies." Indeed, ideology and deception can also create problems under the standard view of democracy as a particular venue for political decision-making.

Democracy, Development, and the State

Although considerations of liberalism call for restraint in the exercise of power by the sovereign, development economists have not fully taken up how modalities of democratic decision-making relate to the process of development.[24] On the contrary, democracy is often seen as being at odds with enlightened policymaking and administration. Lee Kuan Yew of Singapore has stated the view, for example, that political and civic participation in the policy process hampers progress because the ability of the rulership to select the appropriate policy without the interference of party-politics is jeopardized (Daniloff 2000). Here, democracy, vaguely defined but associated with greater personal freedom and regular "free and fair" elections, is seen as a luxury that developing nations can ill afford.

How is democracy related to development? The term "democracy" in particular is so much invoked in political rhetoric that we scarcely stop to reflect on its meaning. As is usually implied, democracy is merely a matter of voting for representatives to parliament. Such an elected central government has as few prospects for encouraging development as any centralized system.[25]

Democracy, if it is to be associated with development, must be further refined from its usual conception as a centralized forum for decision-making based on simple majorities of elected representatives. A system of democratic governance properly refers to various facilities, as conjoined with particular issues of collective action, where problem-solving individuals work out arrangements precedent to mutual exchange. Democracy is grounded in the covenantal character of constitutional choice. It refers to associative institutions crafted in such a way as to help citizens come together to solve problems of collective action in each of various exigencies, so as to enable each to more fully realize their potential for adaptive well-being. The rules conditioning these forums then refer to norms discouraging coercion while encouraging participation, contestation, debate, and consensus.

Democracy in the service of development refers in the first place to circumstances where individuals can bring knowledge of their own time and place with respect to the governance of particular arenas of collective action, in association with knowledge of patterns of relationships as can be gained from scientific study. It deals in the second place with the terms or constitutional mechanisms within which such problem-solving units experiment with alternative solutions as well as those norms within which such units associate and compete with other such problem-solving civic enterprises. If democracy is to be consonant with development, we have to come to a more nuanced view of how individuals constitute themselves in order to improve their own well-being. Accepting something called the state in broad terms presents obstacles to intellectual inquiry on how to foster human well-being in each of the many problem contexts within which we find ourselves.

Rather than look at how democracy, as rooted in various institutional contexts, can impose patterns of order associated with relationships of exchange, the postwar framework of development assumes that there is a center of power. Sovereignty must reside somewhere; if reference is made to a democracy, it is vested in parliament.[26] This abstraction of power as being located at one point enables the formation of an abstract body of positive theory that is to be equally applicable to the variety of constitutional contexts it covers.

If a science of development is based on a theory of a unitary state, it will rely on strategies where the rulership exercises domination over others. As such, the potential for democracy, as a strategy for development through creating potentials for conditioned problem-solving within self-governing societies, is eroded. The role accorded to democracy within the postwar view can lead instead—as Alexis de Tocqueville pointed out in concluding *Democracy in America*—to the "sort of despotism democratic nations have to fear."

In fact, Tocqueville (2000) noted that the culture of inquiry and problem-solving that is crucial to a well-functioning democracy is "trampled underfoot" by the ideology of the state as a great nation whose single and central power directly governs the whole community. In such circumstances, he observed, individuals cease to relate to each other and instead see each other as alike in their relationship to the state. Moreover, as individuals come to regard the state as a "sole, simple, providential, and creative power," the rulership, possessing powers over the fate of the subjects of the state, assumes a paternalistic function with the aim of keeping its wards in a state of "perpetual childhood." As Tocqueville put it, "such power does not destroy, but it prevents existence; it does not tyrannize, but it compresses, enervates, extinguishes, and stupefies a people, till each nation is reduced to nothing better than a flock of timid and industrious animals, of which the government is the shepherd."

Friedrich Hayek (1944) revisited the same idea in the context of national economic planning by the state in *The Road to Serfdom*.[27]

Democratic despotism, as Vincent Ostrom (1997: 17) sums up, is a civic disease brought on when individuals give up their involvement in their local affairs and are drawn in instead by the ideology of the state as an all-purpose problem-solving device. "Democracies are in serious difficulties," he concludes, "when a sickness of the people creates a dependency, a form of servitude, in which the people no longer possess the autonomous capabilities to modify their constitutional arrangements and reform their system of government in appropriate ways."

The notion of using democratic principles as means for achieving the realization of human well-being through conditioned interaction in solving problems of collective action is not core to the approach of the postwar development paradigm. Instead, democracy is seen as merely an added normative condition that has to be fitted in to the challenges of rulership and governance. When seen, for example, as implying the free expression of pluralities of opinion through the formation of governing coalitions, democracy is taken to be an impediment to the adoption of optimal policy remedies. Such a viewpoint considers democracy a luxury that only developed nations can afford.

When democracy is seen primarily a means of legitimizing the exercise of sovereign power by the rulership, it stifles the culture of inquiry and civic engagement. A state centered notion of democracy can suffocate intellectual inquiry and public entrepreneurship needed for individuals to exploit their knowledge of time and place and to build up their institutional resources for their expected future adaptive well-being. In this way, a state centered conception of democracy represents an intellectual failure with serious consequences for development.

Development Beyond the State

Development economics within the postwar ambit has depended on a particular vision of the state.[28] Well-developed critiques already address the epistemic competence and the motivations of the agents of this state to carry out this responsibility, challenging the capability of the state as a positive agent for transforming societies.

The bounds implied in the postwar framework, moreover, have the potential to distract, confuse, and discourage critical reflection and practical problem-solving needed for development to occur. They *distract* by relying on general theoretical approaches that, in striving for coherence from the point of view of the rulership, further complicate efforts by individuals to arrive at appropriate bounds within which to come to grips with the exigencies of their own time and place. They *confuse* when, by creating potentials for a language of inquiry to become clouded with ideological palliatives and insipid generalities, rhetoric replaces reason. In addition, by referring to a central problem-solver, they *discourage* local efforts in institutional innovation and conflict resolution as conditioned within democratic norms.

Bounding a study of development within the concept of the state limits intellectual efforts in seeking creative and locally relevant ways by which individuals can realize better their mutual well-being through the exercise of creative potentials. This "intellectual crisis" calls for a science of association that invokes modes of inquiry and artisanship broadly applicable to all human endeavors (V. Ostrom 1997: 217).

If conceptions of development, reliant on the state as an agent for ushering growth, represent an intellectual crisis, the effects of policies associated with this approach have contributed to the failure of institutions as problem-solving devices. We track this link from intellectual crisis to institutional failure in the following chapter.

CHAPTER 5

The State as the Means to Development

D evelopment theory and aid practice in the postwar framework emphasizes the instrumental role of the state in transforming society. One implication of this emphasis is that when a state fails, the postwar development framework fails as well. Resuscitating the state is one way to save this framework. The Good Governance strategy, adopted by the World Bank and the United Nations Development Programme (UNDP) attempts such a rescue. As noted in the following paragraphs, there are several reasons why the importance of institutions was overlooked in the postwar period and reclaimed more recently. This chapter argues, moreover, that the current effort to revive the state through Good Governance is not itself sustainable since it calls for sound administrative practice without adequate attention to how one might craft their institutional underpinnings.

Governance as an Issue in Development

"Governance" and "Institution-Building" have become fashionable terms in the development literature. The World Bank devoted its 1997 *World Development Report*, to the importance of governance to development. Recently, the UNDP earmarked more than a third of its programming budget for governance related activities. Academic interest in these topics has also burgeoned; a review of listings on the *Econlit* database reveals that a flood of articles have emerged in professional journals on the topic of governance and institution-building through the 1990s to the present.[1]

The World Bank initially acknowledged the relevance of governance to development in a 1989 report, *Sub-Saharan Africa: From Crisis to Sustainable*

Growth. This report showed that carefully considered economic policies have not had the expected developmental impact in sub-Saharan Africa because many of the states in the region lacked the capacity to govern effectively. The World Bank has since supported interventions to promote the governance needed to enhance the capacity of the state in sub-Saharan Africa and elsewhere. It has recommended training, providing resources, and restructuring administrative rules and procedures to spur a more effective state apparatus (World Bank 1997).

Development and the State

Development economics in the aftermath of the Second World War—as influenced by contemporary trends in democratic socialism and Keynesian economics—was seized with the idea of rapid state-led social and economic transformation.[2] Keynes, a leading innovator of this movement, assumed that a ruling elite—in the interest of the public—would carry out macroeconomic policies developed by a priesthood of economists. As adapted into the framework of development, this idea involved the state formulating the "right" policies and faithfully executing them. Other pioneers in development economics, including Rosenstein-Rodan, Nurske, Scitovsky, and Hirschman emphasized the intervention of states, in the face of market failure, to control the allocation of resources and to guide investment.[3]

The idea of the state-led development was also central to models of growth, where growth was portrayed a mechanical process, governed by certain factors of production and the laws of production. Kuznets (1971) considered that the capital oriented development experience of the industrialized countries could be directly transplanted to the developing world. In the influential Solow (1956) model of growth, national output in a closed economy was taken as a function of homogenous labor and homogenous capital, with per capita national output then determined by the capital-labor ratio. (See also Solow 1988.) The argument ran that the returns on capital would be higher in the developing world where capital was scarcer in relation to other factors of production.

As perceived, the constraint facing states in the developing world was that they did not possess the resources to acquire the capital to stimulate this growth. The role of aid then was to cover this domestic resource gap through an injection of external capital in order to release domestic economic growth—what Rostow (1969) referred to as "take-off." Chenery and Strout (1966) noted that during the initial stages of development, aid was required to bridge the difference between capital investment and domestic savings—the internal gap—and the shortfall needed to finance the necessary increase in imports—the external gap.[4]

These initial formulations of development and development assistance, thus, relied on the state to usher development through policy implementation and capital accumulation.

Institutions Overlooked

Aside from the humanitarian concern to uplift conditions in the poorer parts of the world, development aid has and has always had other requisite motivations. *First*, the cold war bipolarity cast the provision of international development assistance within the dynamics of that strategic environment, involving military capabilities. Aid was seen as one way of securing geopolitical alliances—and to that extent, the institutional aspects of third world development were not seen as significant. An egregious example of such strategic aid-provision was that offered to the Siad Barre regime in Somalia.[5] The subsequent collapse of that state and the resulting civil strife and famine are related to the effects of cold war politics.

A *second* reason for a lack of interest in matters institutional relates to the commercial motivations of aid. Agents of donor countries use funds derived from broad based taxation to support their own particular domestic industrial and service lobbies by enabling poor countries to purchase or finance the purchase of capital goods and consultancy services (Jones 1995). While the advancing theory in development economics, with its emphasis on capital accumulation and technical expertise, provided the cover for rent-seeking activities in donor countries, there was little apparent interest or demand for any corresponding theory on the sustainability of such capital acquisitions on the part of aid recipients. There was also little demand for theoretical development on institutional or governance issues on the part of the agents of the recipient countries. One reason may be that greater political capital (or, in some cases, bigger bribes) was to be gained in procuring and inaugurating shiny new projects than in maintaining them.

Third, international development assistance agencies avowedly did not want to get involved in the domestic politics of recipient countries; rhetorically, development was cast as a technical rather than a political issue. Donors claimed that it was not their business to tell sovereign states how to run their affairs or to make judgments about the kind of political system in which development assistance was given (Kilby 1999).

Finally, the growth of a development-industrial complex also played a role. When their colonial possessions were still under their control, countries such as Britain and France invested significantly in their administration and infrastructure. These investments in governance and infrastructure benefited and subsidized those domestic businesses that had invested in producing in the colonies, what was in the main, raw commodities for export and further processing (Cooper 1998).

With independence, most new polities adopted the outward constitutional forms of the erstwhile imperial power, inheriting the administrative norms previously exercised by the officers of the colonial civil service (Hicks 1961). Most newly independent countries from the 1940s through the 1960s themselves were occupied, as a first order of business in nation-building, with setting up institutes or schools of public administration to replace the posts vacated by colonial officers (some of which were funded by donors). There was, however, little need to rethink governance and institution building.

Among the concerns of the withdrawing colonial powers, were the sunk investments in capital left behind. Browne (1997) notes that "independence encouraged new bilateral donors to build aid programmes as a continuation of their colonial obligations." Among these were obligations to their own domestic lobbies—a key rationale behind the establishment of the British Overseas Development Administration.[6]

Institutions Rediscovered

Events since 1990 or so have however motivated a reassessment of the role of institutions and governance in development.[7] This new interest can be traced to three factors.

First, with the demise of the Soviet Union, the motivation to use development aid as a strategic tool in cold war geopolitics waned in significance. To be sure, Western donors could now attach explicit political conditions to their aid directed at the third world recipients without fear of losing their clients to the Soviet camp (Collier 1997 and 1999).[8] The volatility of newly independent former Soviet Republics—facing transitions to statehood, democracy, and market economies—and other similar transition economies of the former second world, also heightened interest among western donors in their political and economic stabilization (Browne and Pflaumer 1996).

Second, the commercial interests of many donor country firms in recipient countries evolved, particularly in wake of advances in production management and communications technology. Globalization of production processes—where parts are produced at various locations for cost reasons and assembled using "just in time" techniques—as well as the offshore outsourcing phenomenon have created a new need for reliable physical and governance infrastructure at those remote sites to facilitate the coordination required. A stable framework of local laws and labor practices are needed, as well as the necessary physical infrastructure to convey reliably these products to the next stage of global assembly or distribution for sale.[9]

A prominent symptom of this change in production has been the rise in Foreign Direct Investment (FDI). Indeed, FDI has eclipsed traditional aid as a tool of economic development in East Asia and elsewhere.[10] Multinational firms operating production facilities in developing countries see it in their common interest to lobby for support aid in areas of governance and infrastructure. The shift to globalized production and rise of FDI has in turn created more demand for an institutional component to development theory.

Finally, the infrastructure of governance that many developing countries had inherited at independence eroded over time, creating a greater awareness of the institutional components of development. Political destabilization through such things as military coups and excessive bureaucratization and top-heavy administrative practices have marked the postcolonial experience in many developing countries; the patterns of public sector vendibility, lack of accountability, and lackluster improvements in well-being that have resulted have made their populations restive.[11]

Moreover, even as the decline of traditional forms of aid has led to fewer opportunities to harvest rents, rulers of some recipient states have found themselves at a competitive disadvantage in attracting foreign investment. Consequently, these same rulers have become more open to reform in spheres that might have otherwise been delimited based on arguments of sovereignty (Rivera-Batiz 2000).

These events have led to reorientation of the interests of western donors who dominate the policymaking boards of major development organizations, as well as those of the representatives of recipient states, and hence to the policy predisposition of these development organizations themselves.[12] In turn, this has drawn increased attention to ongoing efforts at scholarship in such areas as New Institutional Economics, which emphasizes the importance of stable institutions for the development of a market economy, neoliberal arguments concerning the virtues of a slim and efficient bureaucracy, as well as soul searching to explain the failures of fifty years of organized development effort.[13]

Good Governance: In Practice and Prospect

If the relevance of governance for sustainable development has been recognized, how has this translated into theory and practice? A key approach taken by the World Bank and the UNDP is to identify elements associated with effective government in western polities and to strengthen the capacity of the governments of developing nations in each of these respects. Within these approaches, the role of the state in correcting perceived market failures and in directing economic growth and human development is left unchallenged.

Box 5.1 Programming Governance

The 1997 *World Development Report* holds that strengthening governance increases the potential of the state to carry out its role. Governance projects, thus, seek to improve the quality of central policymaking and coordination, discipline policymakers to adopt expert advice, upgrade administrative systems, and increase the motivation and capability of civil servants to comply and carryout polices so established.

To this end, projects relating to governance typically provide for:

- Training economists and other policy innovators to improve the quality of advice offered to policymakers;
- Training legislators to follow parliamentary procedure and sensitize them to social and economic issues;
- Supporting statistical agencies to augment data inputs to the policymaking process and enhance transparency by disseminating information on economic variables;
- Training civil servants in administration and bureaucratic management in order to create an enabling environment for the private sector and to enhance "delivery systems" for policy decisions;
- Training judges and other legal professionals to foster greater adherence to due process;
- Purchasing office-automation equipment to increase efficiency and to provide access to modern electronic information systems;
- Funding of voter registration and elections;
- Supporting civil society and non-governmental organizations so that they may serve as intermediaries between "the People" and "the State."

According to the World Bank's 1997 *World Development Report*, which is devoted to the issue of governance, the state's proper role is to develop good policies and to foster the institutional environment where they can be implemented. The state is seen to be that entity which establishes and adjudicates the economic, social, and political rules and regulations. It is also a major player in all these spheres. Its function is to furnish active macroeconomic management, to provide or ensure the provision of basic education, health, and environmental protection, and to render a fertile institutional soil within which markets can grow.

The UNDP (1998) similarly views the state as on one hand establishing and maintaining a stable and effective legal and regulatory framework while at the same time actively engaged in such things as managing the macroeconomic variables, providing public services, and protecting the rights of the vulnerable. The purpose of governance aid is thus to strengthen the capacity of governments in each of these respects.

Is Good Governance Sustainable?

The immediate appeal of putting to practice projects and programs that enhance the features of good governance is that by making government work better, they promise to enhance the sustainability of other developmental initiatives. If poor implementation, a lack of interest in maintenance, and corruption and political venality undermine development, then recognizing and improving the administrative setting within which public policies are carried out would seem to improve the prospects for success in development.

In the World Bank's view, Good Governance is maintained through the proper conduct and interaction of the policymaking and administrative organs of the state, along with the statistical and auditing services, the judiciary, and finally, civil society organizations.[14] The Bank advocates smaller and smarter states where hiring is based on established procedure and training is provided in policy analysis and economic management (World Bank 1989a, 1989b, 1991; Landell-Mills and Serageldin 1991). It holds that auditing, accounting, and information dissemination procedures are to be developed so that individuals can better judge the performance of their government (World Bank 1992). Statistical services are also to be upgraded since otherwise, it is argued, society will not have enough information about the activities and accomplishments of the state to hold it accountable for its actions. An improved legal system—emphasizing due process—is to facilitate greater transparency in government. This entails, variously, redrawing laws on property rights, bankruptcy, and trade, as well as training and supporting judges, lawyers, and other court officials. In addition, the World Bank (1997) endorses civil society organizations as intermediaries between "the government" and "the people." These groups are expected to provide a countervailing force to the power of the state and to hold it accountable within certain, if unspecified, regularized procedural constraints.[15]

Decentralization is also recognized an organizational feature of good governance. The World Bank and the UNDP (1998) refer to decentralization as a means of improving governance, though enthusiasm for decentralization is diluted by the consideration of the implied loss of control by the state over policy and public administration.[16] Fiscal decentralization, for example, is seen to conflict with the core state responsibility of managing macroeconomic variables. Devolution of political authority to lower levels of government, it is feared, will lead to regional disparities in service provisions, misallocation of resources, and inadequate policy guidance.[17]

Given these reservations, the World Bank and UNDP vision of reform in governance relies heavily on the professionalization of public servants; although a perusal of the 1997 *World Development Report* leaves the reader impressed with the breadth of topics considered, the prototype for action left standing at the end of the day is one where efficient delivery of public goods takes place in correspondence with the latest advances in information technology and policy advice through a centrally consolidated provision of the services by the state. If the public good in question is good governance, then it is again the responsibility of the state to put into place the necessary conditions to upgrade its own credibility, consistency, and predictability.

Good Governance attempts to address an *institutional gap* by identifying the characteristics of good governance found in the organization of the polities of the developed world and by replicating some of them on a piecemeal basis in the polities of developing world. This approach fails to appreciate that these characteristics are themselves a part of an overall order generated through the conditioned interactions of individuals acting purposefully within the bounds of certain fundamental levels of social and political rules and institutions. *Good Governance*—in the sense of an operational strategy—does not diagnose what institutional factors gives rise to the observed characteristics of good governance—in the sense of a desirable state of affairs.

Thus, Good Governance is not institutionally robust. It continues to be rooted in certain essentialist views of "the State" and "the People," where the former entity gathers data, diagnoses problems, develops solutions and implements them upon a passive populace; people here are more subjects and less citizens. Left unexplained consequently is how the conflicts inherent in the state acting as rule-maker, referee, and player may be resolved. Indeed, Good Governance as proposed continues to rely on the postwar development paradigm in considering the dichotomy between the development of policy by enlightened social scientists and implementation by a rulership, with a presumption that development will occur when the each of the many characteristics associated with it are more faithfully individually replicated and assembled. It does not adequately address how to embed the checks and balances within a constitutional system so as to maintain good government through the vicissitudes of history and politics.

Toward an Institutional Foundation for Development

The program of Good Governance reflects an important change in the postwar view—from one where the state is an omniscient and benevolent agent for positive social impact to one where the state is an imperfect agent for change, but one that is subject to improvement through training in policy analysis and administration. Even so, Good Governance does not alter the basic state-based framework of development. In the previous chapter, we reviewed some problems related to the *motivations* of the agents of the state and the use of *knowledge* needed to make time and place relevant policy decisions. A third added consideration relates to *institutions and processes*.

Standard approaches in development rely on a state as a means to put into place characteristics—including, now, those of Good Governance—associated with advanced development. This gap-filling approach fails to appreciate that the features that we associate with advanced societies, and find wanting in less developed ones, are the results and manifestations of processes of interaction and that only changes in these patterns of interactions can produce patterns of outcomes alternative to those now experienced; replicating these outward characteristics without understanding the processes that bring them about may well yield counterintuitive and counter-intentional outcomes. Attempts to change the outward characteristics that are the result of a rule-bounded process can alter the involved institutions in an unconstrained way. Approaches to development that seek to use the coercive power of the state to replicate characteristics of developed countries therefore are prone to not be sustainable.

Good government is required for development but such government need not be synonymous with postwar conceptions of the state in development. Good government, we will argue, emerges rather from reflection and choice in designing levels of commitments among problem-solving citizens who, within their various and overlapping communities, are accountable to each other. A constitution of development then must deal with how such a robust and self-sustaining *infrastructure* can be crafted. We need to rethink the *superstructure* of the state as a central ideological feature of development.

Individuals, in the real world, attempt to improve their own well-being within the constraints framed by the complex of existing institutional structures. Legal processes and legislated constraints form a part of these complex social rules. While the operations of governments are typically set up, if only formally in some cases, in terms of laws and procedures, the structure of the prevailing social capital draws, as well, on a panoply of widely understood, reliable, and recognizable institutional regularities. These may be the intentional products of attempts at creating order. More often, they derive spontaneously from the way individuals interpret the actions and interactions of others within a community of understanding that is as bounded by shared values, norms, and perceptions.

While organizations are palpable and development characteristics are subject to measurement, shared values and mutual understandings underpinning institutions are invisible. Yet, the scope for humans to realize their well-being through the exercise of their creative potentials rests critically on appreciating these invisible institutional underpinnings of social order. Unless the organization of governance is rooted in these ontological underpinnings, it will fail to take on institutional significance.

*   *   *

The focus on "Good Governance" is a positive development in that it highlights the limits of the state as a device for development. As we have seen, however, the approach (of the World Bank and others) reflecting this new emphasis is not sufficiently "bottom-up" or institutionally well-grounded and therefore not likely to be sustainable. Good government requires more, as we discover next in part II.

PART 2

Institutions and Development

CHAPTER 6

The Constitutional Foundations of Development

Freedom, Amartya Sen (1999a) argues, is a means of realizing an improvement in the general welfare as well as a goal of economic and social life itself. Freedom is key if humans are to exercise their innovative potentials to realize and fulfill their sense of well-being. The way we constitute our relationships—through a focus on the rules of association and exchange—bears on our freedoms and, hence, on our prospective well-being. The constitutional challenge, in this regard, rests in harmonizing this freedom within an ordered system of association.

State Governance and Constitutional Governance

In part I, we saw that state governance represents one vision of a constitutional system where the rulers exercise unique prerogatives to set out and enforce laws regulating social and commercial interaction. A key rationale of this approach, set out famously by Thomas Hobbes, is that deference to a sovereign frees individuals from conflict arising from competing claims. There is nothing per se wrong with state governance as a system of association so long as a state can function as the collective-action instrument of its subjects. However, a centralizing state can deprive its subjects of important capabilities when the exercise of rulership prerogatives is not effectively constrained. Such a weakly constituted state, we argue, undermines development.

Constitutional governance, in contrast to state governance, is consonant with citizens addressing their common needs through the freedom to integrate their actions with those of others within crafted rules and innovated institutional arrangements. Such efforts in self-governance can be effective when constrained through mutual accountability cultivated within local communities of understanding. Here, "local" refers to a particular arena of collective action, and the term "communities of understanding" relates to shared values, norms, and perceptions that bind citizens within a problem arena. In this context, the challenge of constitutional design relates to the articulation of an overall *system* of interlinked problem-solving arenas. Such a constitutional system draws on the constraints implied in the institutional understandings shared among citizens within a particular problem arena while nested within broader normative frames of reference.[1]

This ontology of constitutional governance differs from the experience of societies in much of the developing world where Western Constitutions were often used as models for the formal organization of the state.[2] Unanchored to local communities of understanding, these transplanted charters have often failed to take on a larger institutional significance—most often fostering top-down states rather than bottom-up organizations. One result has been inadequately constrained state governance, offering weak prospects for both freedom and development.

This experience shows that the future of effective development through good government does not lie in coaxing particular constitutional models to work in transplanted settings. Nor, for that matter, does it rest with returning societies to an imagined Shangri-La precolonial past. As a practical matter, it depends instead in advancing systems of interaction—the constitutional rules of the game—that simultaneously draw strength from and build upon prevailing institutional understandings.

This chapter draws together the analytical foundations of constitutional governance. Amartya Sen's recent emphasis on "freedom" as a goal of economic life as well as a means for citizens to associate with each other in realizing their capabilities provides a segue to Alexis de Tocqueville's analysis of constitutionally grounded development. This leads us to two complementary methodological approaches to constitutional governance—the *covenantal* basis emphasized by Vincent Ostrom and the *contractarian* approach set out by James Buchanan.

Sen's Development as Freedom

In *Development as Freedom*, Amartya Sen urges development theorists and practitioners away from a sole preoccupation with neoclassical formalisms and poverty measurements. The way forward, he notes, lies more in conceptualizing the problem of underdevelopment as one intrinsically related to the lack of freedom. Sen holds his approach to be paradigm altering.[3]

Sen holds that freedom is related to development in two ways. He notes that freedom—the potential for the exercise of reflection and choice—is the ultimate *goal* of economic life while also the most efficient *means* of realizing general welfare. Following this distinction, Sen maintains that social arrangements, such as the market, expand individual freedoms, while individual freedoms, such as economic liberties, serve to make social arrangements (like the market) more effective. Conversely, he finds that economic "unfreedoms" prompt social "unfreedoms," and vice versa.

If capability is a kind of freedom—enabling the achievement of different outcomes through permitting the combining and arranging of available of resources—poverty, as a deprivation of such capability, emerges from a denial of such opportunities. Thus, when deprivations of political expression limit such capabilities, economic freedom is also compromised. The level of development, concludes Sen, depends not only on traditional measures of industrialization and progress, but on the level of freedoms people enjoy, as derived from their social and economic arrangements and from the political and civil rights they enjoy.

Sen's arguments provide three important openings in the study of development: First, they loosen the emphasis on measures of national wealth and other aggregate indicators of poverty as the analytical point of departure. This frees development theory from being preoccupied with data driven policy remedies. Development can now be taken as more a matter of the acquisition and exercise of freedom by individuals in relation to each other than one of creating and administering clever policy interventions; within the Freedom perspective, Sen (1999a: 11) points out, the poor of the world "need not be seen primarily as passive recipients of benefits of cunning development programs."

Second, they highlight the importance of institutions. Sen (1999a: 5) notes that a proper consideration of issues relating to poverty has to include how individuals, given freedom to associate, can form institutional arrangements that enhance their capabilities: "The institutional arrangements for these opportunities are also influenced by the exercise of people's freedoms, through the liberty to participate in social choice and in making of public decisions that impel the progress of these opportunities." In this way, Sen admonishes us to look beyond the rhetoric of "free markets" on one hand or the terror of authoritarianism on the other to consider the institutional foundations of development.

Finally, Sen's approach draws attention to the importance of values. Sen (1999a: 10) points out that values mediate the exercise of freedom and are therefore necessary for development. At the same time, such values are themselves influenced through processes of public decision-making and civic engagement. Public participation in valuational debates is thus a part of the exercise of democracy and responsible social choice. Sen argues that the freedom to engage in such political discussion is itself conducive to development. As such, he urges us to go beyond traditional measures of utility, income, and wealth, and to return to the ancient and classical roots of the analysis of development for an understanding of the meaning of value and its relation to human well-being.

Sen has opened the study of development to the importance of freedom, institutions, and values. This opening requires follow-up on how freedom can be secured, how institutions can be crafted, and how values can be incorporated within systems of economic and political exchange. If well-being is secured through freeing the individual to be involved in and making decisions regarding his or her own life, how are we to conceive of a compatible system of government?

Freedom, Democracy, and Constitutional Order

In considering development within a constitutional perspective, we begin with some principles drawn from Alexis de Tocqueville's analysis of constitutional governance in the United States.[4] As Tocqueville plainly noted, his analysis of governance was not to describe a phenomenon unique to the United Sates—made possible in part by exceptional historical circumstances—but rather to develop a deeper understanding of the principles underlying good government so as to inform a process of constitutional reform in his native France.

In *Democracy in America*, Tocqueville considered whether a society could be created where its members govern themselves on their own behalf, without recourse to a supreme center of authority. He concluded that this would depend on citizens acquiring an "art and science of association" such that they could, at their own initiative, design, construct, operate, and modify patterns of associative relationships, required to address their own needs. This skill, concluded Tocqueville, would only emerge within the framework of *constitutional democracies*, where the costs of engaging in such forms of public entrepreneurship meet or are surpassed by the expected benefits that come from collective action in problem-solving. Tocqueville's method of analysis is thus very relevant to the contemporary challenge of good government and development.

Tocqueville's Analysis of Constitutional Governance

Tocqueville (2000: Chapter VI), in considering the constitution of France in the mid-nineteenth century in relation to the turmoil in contemporary political and economic events, sought to answer the puzzle of how local autonomy, needed to marshal local knowledge and local understandings to the resolution of local problems, could be reconciled with the need for coherence through a uniformity of law across the nation. After all, if local officials were answerable only to the local electorate, would this not lead to the dissolution of the larger polity?

Since Hobbes' *Leviathan*, the classic response to the problem of order in society has been to vest a sovereign with a monopoly on legal authority. However, Tocqueville (2000) found order in America, though in the absence of a state as known in France—a society that "goes along by itself," as he called it. In resolving his puzzle, Tocqueville sought to determine the principles upon which local autonomy and national coherence were reconciled in the United States. In doing so, Tocqueville was careful to distinguish the analytics underpinning good government in the United States from the unique historical circumstances of United States. His purpose, after all, was to distill the institutional underpinnings of democracy in America in order to apply them to contemporary France.

Tocqueville observed that the American government was built from the bottom up. The colonists, he found, first constituted themselves within local units of self-governance and only then joined themselves together within regional forms of government. The idea of a national government was to come only much later. He saw the fundamental building block of American democracy in township governance, particularly as manifested in New England.

What in turn made township governance work was the prevailing culture of problem-solving, engrained in the habits and attitudes of the population. These mores, Tocqueville observed, enabled people to associate freely and to deal with public needs as they emerged. He noted that the basis for a democracy, and the social stability and progress it afforded, rests in the shared beliefs and traditions of meeting, debating, and settling local affairs locally. To Tocqueville, these mores contributed more to the maintenance of a democratic republic than the prevailing laws or other unique circumstances of the New World.[5]

How was administrative and policymaking autonomy found at the local level reconciled with the need for an overall coherence? Tocqueville noted that local problem-solving communities were interlinked through systems of regional governance. In addition, day-to-day development and maintenance of such local concerns as schools, roads, and public services were organized within the local community, though constrained within the basic standards for rule-making set up at the state level. Representing institutional precommitments, the governments of the states and ultimately the federal government provided, in principle, a way to deal with more broadly shared problems of collective action as well as to link and set conditions within which local problem-solving efforts could proceed.[6]

Tocqueville noted that constitutional design at these more comprehensive levels was critical to maintaining the viability of township democracy. Although the government of the United States was developed on ideals of federalism, he found that the governments of the states at the time of his visit were largely not so constituted.[7] The United States Constitution, based on design principles of competitive checks and balances, was confined in the main to resolving problems that could arise among the states of the union. At the time of Tocqueville's visit in the 1830s, however, these principles of federalism did not apply to the constitutions of some states—as regards the problem-solving relationships between citizens of cities, towns, and counties, and similarly for the charters of these jurisdictions with respect to their localities (Tocqueville 2000: Book I, Chapter 5).

In fact, constitutions of many states were based more on simple principles of majority rule and it was in this that Tocqueville anticipated the greatest danger to American democracy. Given that state constitutions provided for few checks on the tyranny of the majority, he foresaw that legislators, executives, and the judiciary could become dominated by majority coalitions. Though nominally democratic, governance at the state level, he feared, would become centralized and the strength of democracy in America, as derived from its local problem-solving traditions, would become jeopardized.

Such dangers for American democracy, still nascent at the time of Tocqueville's visits, were to manifest themselves in the Boss Rule and Machine Politics a few decades laser—symptoms of the "state-monopoly" tendencies to which Tocqueville objected.[8] It is worth noting that it was not until the institutional innovations of the Progressive Movement—in restructuring the constitutions of the states based on principles of federalism and checks and balances—that many of these symptoms of poor governance came to be relieved.[9]

Constitutional Governance and Early United States Development

Tocqueville (2000: Book I, Chapter 5) concluded that the absence of uniform rules ensuing from traditions in local problem-solving, although untidy and a nuisance in some respects, was more than made up by the increased social vitality, creativity, and self-reliance among the citizenry:

> In America, the social force behind the state is much less well regulated, less enlightened, and less wise, but it is a hundred times more powerful than in Europe. Without doubt, there is no other country on earth where people take such great efforts to achieve social prosperity. I know of no other people who have founded so many schools or such efficient ones, or churches more in touch with the religious needs of the inhabitants, or municipal roads better maintained. So it is no good looking in the United States for perfection of administrative procedures; what one does find is a picture of power, somewhat wild perhaps, but robust, and a life liable to mishaps but full of striving and animation.

This vitality and creativity is an essential engine for development. Tocqueville's commentary underscores that unless systems of administration are rooted on understanding how problem-solving individuals can constitute themselves to address their need to work collectively, endogenously sustained development will not occur. Coherence, in other words, has critically to be achieved from the point of view of the citizen in relation to his fellow problem solvers, rather than from the standpoint of the sovereign's advisors and administrators.

Tocqueville's insights on the significance of constitutional democracy as an alternative to the state and as a foundation for social prosperity and the efficient production and provision of public goods and services require careful attention for their relevance to contemporary governance and underdevelopment (Gellar, 2005). Recall that Tocqueville's purpose in writing *Democracy in America* was not to describe a historical phenomenon unique to time and place, but rather to advance the constitutional development of France by elaborating a general "science of association" drawn from best practice principles of governance as observed in the United States. To meet today's challenge of development, Tocqueville's analytics need to be elaborated and made more systematic within a framework of inquiry that, through integrating political, economic, and behavioral studies, illuminates how individuals may realize their adaptive potential via strengthening and ordering the ways in which they relate to one another.[10]

With this understanding, we now turn to two complementary ways of coming to terms with how systems of collective action can be constituted. The first, a *covenantal* basis, has been emphasized by Vincent Ostrom. The second is James Buchanan's *contractarian* approach.

Associative Foundations of Constitutional Systems of Government

Individualism and Communalism

For individuality to take on meaning, it must be expressed in contexts where we relate to each other as we cope with life's problems. In such situations, we each can bring our intelligence, our individuality, and our particular competence to bear. At the same time, interactions in the public realm are conditioned by prevailing structures of explicit and implicit social rules. Thus, the potential for freedom through the exercise of individual capability varies with the structure (or constitution) of these social arrangements.

Vincent Ostrom (1997: 117) notes in this regard that "it is important that we attempt to clarify the human condition and how that condition establishes essential foundations for what it would mean to become self-governing." He observes that systems of collective action cohere when they are drawn from communities of understandings. Communities of understanding, in turn, are founded on subjective considerations applicable to moral sentiments and social feelings.

Further, given that individuality takes on meaning only in the context of social existence, the problem-solving capacity of a society and the potential for fruitful self-governance depends on its citizens distinguishing between selfishness and "self-interest, rightly understood"—a term Ostrom borrows from Tocqueville, meaning a proper understanding of one's own position formed by broader considerations that take into account the interests of others (Ibid.).

Any effort to calculate a broader self-interest requires individuals to take into account not just the interests of others but also a deeper appreciation of the point of view likely to be adopted by others whose contributions are important to achieving one's own goals. Thus, individuals need a sense of sympathy to understand better how others might react to an opportunity to join in collective efforts. Sympathy, in this sense, is essential to effective collective action. Covenanting and contracting can proceed out of a common understanding based on shared sympathies.

"Sympathy" as a Foundation for Systems of Human Relationships

The behavioral and ontological foundations of constitutional governance have been long noted, with Adam Smith, David Hume, and Thomas Hobbes each finding that the basis for successful human organization lies in our capacity to understand others.

Adam Smith (2000), in *The Theory of Moral Sentiments* invoked the medium of the "Impartial Spectator" as a way of bringing our feeling and reasoning to bear on the problem of cooperation. The balance between Prudence, Benevolence, and Justice, needed to overcome this problem, noted Smith, is obtained only by our capacity to imagine and develop genuine feelings for others. The well-being of individuals in society depends therefore on a balance between our care for our own welfare and our care for the welfare of others, as tempered by the rules by which our freedoms are secured and coercion circumscribed. Thus, we depend on our *sympathies*—our concern for the regard of others and our sense of fellow feeling—as well as on our *intellects* to devise a set of rules—a calculus of consent—upon which we can live in peace.[11]

David Hume (1999) in his essays on *Human Understanding* similarly noted that we are able to develop successively more complex rules of conduct through our identification with each other's feelings. As such, he distinguished between "natural virtues" and "artificial virtues"—where the former are those impelled by propensities such as sympathy by which we make the pleasures and pains of others our own and where the latter are a consequence of human contrivance.

As Ostrom (1997: 19) sums up, Hume observed that "human beings can construct patterns of relationships as artifices in which social sentiments such as friendship, respect, affection, trust, fraternity, and collegiality might give a binding quality to human relationships that are conducive to felicity, happiness, and well-being."

Thomas Hobbes' (1972) essay, *Of Man* also begins with the proposition that humans can use their own cognitive resources to understand how others think and feel. In addition, Hobbes observed, humans are able to develop and employ their foresight and imagination to anticipate and prompt events. In this way, humans constantly and persistently seek to use what they recognize as their present means to achieve future desired ends. In resolving this quest to adapt, humans rely on peaceful associations with others. Hobbes held that conditions of such a peace relied on invoking the Golden Rule: "*Do not that to another, which thou would not have done to thyself.*" Cooperation is made possible when, by placing ourselves in the other's shoes, we may cancel out thought and action that are purely self-interested.[12]

Sympathy is Necessary but not Sufficient

Striving to cooperate, obliged solely as it is by one's conscience, may not always compel one's actions. In the absence of more explicit constraints, surmised Hobbes, individuals in possession of their natural abilities, and driven to improve their position by exploiting available means, would find themselves in a state of nature. Here, each would be free to attack as well as defend. Unconstrained competition for scarce resources would lead to conflict—a state of war of "every man against every man"; self-interest leads to misery. Hobbes therefore concluded that for order corresponding to the Golden Rule to be realized, a Sovereign, representing a unity of power, is needed to uphold a unity of law.

Hobbes was correct in noting that sympathy alone is insufficient for a robust system of human relationships. Yet, this does not mean that we must rely on the mercy, initiative, and capability of a center of authority—a Sovereign—to create coherence in society. Hobbes argument is critically flawed, notes Ostrom (1991), in that it does not consider the capability of speech and the use of language by humans to craft solutions to problems of order within their communities.

Language in the Constitution of Order

If sympathy is essential in forming human relationships, constitutional democracy, built on a network of such relationships, is made possible through the medium of speech and language. In this regard, Smith and Hume recognized that language, through giving expression to the moral sentiments, enables a standard of justice to emerge in the mediation of human relationships. As Hume (1966) wrote in *An Enquiry Concerning the Principles of Morals*,

> The distinction, therefore, between the species of sentiment [i.e., sympathy versus other base passions] being so great and evident, language must soon be moulded upon it and must invent a peculiar set of terms in order to express those universal sentiments of censure and approbation which arise from humanity or from views of general usefulness and its contrary. Virtue and Vice become known; morals are recognized; certain general rules are framed of human conduct, and behavior; such measures are expected of men in such situations. This action is conformable to an abstract rule; the other contrary. And by such universal principles are the particular sentiments of self-love frequently controlled and limited.

Human sentiment, language, and morals, all intrinsically tied together, form the basis of common understanding within a problem-solving community. Collective action is facilitated when there is mutual understanding among members of a group based on certain shared perspectives on the nature of the problem as is particular and relevant to that time and place. The notion of a *community of understanding* relates to this commonly bounded system of conceptualizing reality.

Language helps bind these communities of understanding through the articulation and communication of logical thought related to the process of problem-solving. It serves as an instrument for expressing concepts and for relating symbols and relationships central to cooperative coexistence. As such, it becomes the basis for stipulating the rules by which we come to think of, expect, and appreciate the behavior of others.

In all, sympathy, combined with an advanced capacity for language, enables the creation of the culture of problem-solving.[13] This culture is constituted by the knowledge shared in the community about the nature of the common problem uniquely confronted and the understandings that humans can develop of each other in jointly addressing this problem. It is further identified by its articulation through language in the rules and agreements that arise from such understandings. Finally, it is manifested in the patterns of activity that emerge through the action and interaction of humans within these rules and crafted constraints.

The Covenantal Basis of Constitutional Democracy

Constitutional democracy, as a framework for development, relies on humans interacting within contexts where their own knowledge and understandings of each other in relation to the problem encountered gain significance. The particular ways in which individuals relate to one and other, as reflected in language, is rooted in their own cultural traditions even as sympathy serves as the common basis by which rapport is established. People everywhere attempt to cope with the needs of life through association with others; communal arrangements as we have noted are a universal feature of human existence. If individuals are to realize an improvement in their own welfare, these communal arrangements within which they interact must be grounded in the indigenous moral and cultural realities that serve to bind the community.

Tocqueville, in appreciating the constitutional meaning of township governments of New England, noted that they arose from shared religious values; Judeo-Christian ethics, in this case, provided the foundations for shared mores. As such, the constitutional foundations of good government in the United States emerged from many of its own traditions in covenanting.[14] The process of covenanting imbued the citizen with the responsibility and moral commitment to struggle with others in recognizing and overcoming commonly confronted problems. Involving a deeper level of mutual understanding beyond merely its specific terms, a covenant thus obliged the citizen to participate in a sympathetic effort to resolve problems through respect for each other's standing. It was in this respect that Tocqueville considered religion for Americans to be "the first of their political institutions" even though religion took "no direct part in the government of society."

Daniel Elazar (1995), in this regard, has drawn attention to the relevance of such covenanting and covenantal relationships to the understanding of constitutions. (See also Elazar 1988) The term "federalism" he noted, derives after all from the Latin-root for "covenant"—*foedus*. A federal constitutional order is thus founded fundamentally on an association of moral communities, each expressing in its own way Hobbes' Golden Rule, and where commitments are made by citizens to engage each other *sympathetically* in efforts at problem-solving. These precepts, as Elazar further noted, are not unique to any particular religious tradition. Indeed, the covenantal basis, required for constitutional democracy, is prevalent in most civilizations.[15] This covenantal basis for association, which is usually found in society, in combination with other approaches to human organization, however, needs to be recognized and drawn on in crafting the foundation of a sustainable constitutional understanding.[16]

In fact, once we identify the context of constitutional choice, these covenantal foundations can be drawn upon explicitly in expressing and crafting rules that are appropriate to specific contexts and particular communities of understanding.

The Logical Foundations of Constitutional Analysis

Methodological Individualism

The Calculus of Consent, Logical Foundations of Constitutional Democracy, coauthored by James Buchanan and Gordon Tullock and published in 1962, provides a complementary introduction to constitutional choice and analysis. In setting out the constitutional foundations of systems of collective action, Buchanan sets out explicitly that the individual is conceptually separable from the community and that an analysis of collective action can be derived from the point of view of the individual's choice calculus. Once the analytical starting point of the autonomous choosing individual is accepted, contends Buchanan, a fruitful examination can be initiated into how a problem-solving community is constituted through choice among rules and of how adaptation takes place within such rules.

The field of Constitutional Political Economy, as since advanced by Buchanan and others, proceeds from this overture. With Methodological Individualism as its foundation, this constitutional approach differentiates among the various levels at which contractual commitments can be made and within which strategies may be undertaken. It further develops for us particular conceptual building blocks and associated terminology needed to come to terms with the relevance of constitutional democracy to the issue of freedom and the problem of underdevelopment.

The Constitutional Level of Analysis

The distinction—choice *within* constraints, as opposed to choice *among* constraints—distinguishes the domain of Constitutional Political Economy (Buchanan 1990). The crafting of constraints in constituting a system of collective action and the actions subsumed within these imply strategies at various rule levels. An analogy can be drawn here to a game of poker where players adopt strategies in attempts to win within the framework of particular rules while, at the same time, possibly entering into side discussions about crafting rule changes in an attempt to improve the game.

The *constitutional* and *sub-constitutional* levels of rules and orders thus refer to a structure of relationships and the patterns of interaction that develop within the confines the particular sets of rules through available strategies in problem-solving. In general, we can conceive of such constitutional and sub-constitutional rules to be nested, with rules that define the arena of action— our analytical focal point—as provisionally accepted or relatively absolute points of reference. "Rational" behavior in associative relationships is so bounded.

The Theory of Constitutional Contract

Buchanan (1991) asks us to consider that in market exchange, the relevant relationship, whether in acts of joint commitment within an ongoing basis or in a particular transaction, takes place between two parties—the buyer and the seller. Here, the "goodness" of the rules of transaction is established through the voluntary nature of the exchange. By contrast, in politics, there is group action with simultaneous exchange among many parties. In ongoing multilateral exchange relationships, such as those within a family, club, or other system of collective action, individuals choose to submit to certain impositions in exchange for benefits they could not otherwise singly realize. To gain the benefits of collective action, we may agree to precommit ourselves by establishing particular contingencies of reinforcement. How can the "goodness" of such corporate relationships be gauged?

Traditional responses to this query have relied on the concept of utility. The Classical Welfare Economics approach to politics centered on the notion that utility could be aggregated. However, it soon became clear that utility could not be in any sense measurable within, or aggregated among persons.[17]

Paretian Welfare Economics attempted an alternate way of comparing problem-solving alternatives without requiring the measurement of utility (Buchanan 1987). An option was considered Pareto efficient if it reflected a situation in which no change could make an individual better-off without some other being made worse-off. Here, "better-off" and "worse-off" were conceived in terms of individuals' utilities, as reflected through choices made. According to the Revealed Preference Approach, if a person, observed by the analyst to be in an initial position, moves to a new position given the opportunity, then the new one is revealed preferred to the old one (Samuelson 1948). If the person chooses not to move, then the initial state is held to be at least as good. The Pareto formulation, while recognizing that values are subjective, is nevertheless not explicit about the context within which evaluations of the same are to be made.

By contrast, for Knut Wicksell—applying himself to a problem in Public Finance—the criterion of efficiency for a system of collective action rested in the evaluations of the individuals involved; each person would assess if the benefits to him or her of a mooted joint action would outweigh the costs to him or her, as perceived (Buchanan 1987: chapter 19). Thus, as Buchanan (1991: chapter 9) expresses it, the Wicksellian Unanimity Criterion holds that

> When a specific expenditure project was presented, a whole array of possible distributions of the required tax bill was also to be presented, with each array estimated to produce revenues sufficient to cover the outlay. The expenditure project

was then to be voted on in the legislature, along with each one of the tax allocations, and when one such combination secured the unanimous approval of the assembly, it was to be adopted. If no single combination received unanimous support, the expenditure project was not to be undertaken and no tax was to be levied.

Wicksell's insight is key in that it leads us to consider that the structure of the decision rules themselves are variable and therefore subject to choice, and that we need not be bound in weighing policy options under an implicitly unchanging rule structure.

However, the strict unanimity condition can lead to a holdout problem, where each interest is motivated to withhold consent until his or her best position is realized. Such a rule can lead to paralysis. In considering such potential for strategic behavior, and the practical difficulties encountered in seeking even near unanimity in every public decision, Buchanan shifts the level of the argument back and adopts the notion, proposed by James Madison, where consensus approaching unanimity is adopted at the constitutional level and majority voting rules are adopted for sub-constitutional collective decision-making. (A cost calculus is involved here in considering alternatives among voting rules themselves.) Conceptual Unanimity therefore implies that collective choice, made at the sub-constitutional level, proceeds within an overall context of shared acknowledgements (or community of understanding) brought about through unanimity in constitutional agreement (Buchanan 1991).

We thus form the basis for individuals to constitute themselves about problems of collective action at any given level—be it local, regional, or more broadly relevant—as oriented upon a general set of unanimously adopted rules and precommitments. A "limited constitution" is extended in this way to various forums of human association with the need to craft rules appropriate for each problem-solving context now made explicit.

In this, there is considered a smaller likelihood of disagreement and a motivation to be fair at the constitutional rulemaking level due to the *veil of uncertainty*. That is, despite their particular theories about the workings of rules through time, rule-makers may still expect to be governed by their own rules in contingencies and ways that they cannot fully anticipate. (As such, this veil grows more opaque as the rules become more general and their application more indefinite (Buchanan and Vanberg 1989).) Coercion is absent if no public initiative is undertaken, except within the overall framework of unanimously and freely accepted rules. If under these circumstances, individuals do not initiate changes to extant rules and institutions, then that situation may be judged to be *Constitutionally Efficient* (Wiseman 1996).

We can now compare Constitutional Efficiency with Pareto Efficiency in terms of the distinction between "constitutional governance" and "state governance." In the former, the values of individuals are given equal weight through unanimity *processes* of approval, whereas in the latter, choice *outcomes* are "compared" equally. That is, while the Constitutional notion places stress on the unanimous or near unanimous adoption of pre-commitments by citizens in the absence of coercion—and while the unanimity condition ensures equal weight to the perceptions of well-being of each of the participating citizens regarding the working properties of rules—the Pareto notion depends on an external evaluation at some point in time of the preferences of subjects without full reference to the institutional context within which such preferences are manifested. The Constitutional approach adopted here therefore appreciates the "goodness" of corporate exchange as emerging from a democratic process within constitutional constraints.

Buchanan's Constitutional Political Economy thus views individuals as capable of choosing to impose constraints on their own behavior, primarily as a part of an exchange in which the freedom of one's own actions are forsaken in return for anticipated benefits from others similarly limiting themselves. Constitutional democracy is logically founded upon a credible and voluntary exchange of commitments based on a calculus of consent. The "goodness" of the social arrangements it fosters is implied within the principle of conceptual unanimity in setting up the rules for such exchange.

Understanding Constitutional Governance

Poverty, as Amartya Sen notes, is reflective of patterns of social order where individuals are not free to realize their adaptive well-being through the exercise of creativity in organizing collective effort. Addressing poverty, thus, requires that we tackle the problem of social order based on the principles of constitutional governance. Vincent Ostrom's emphasis on the need to understand the behavioral and ontological foundations of good government and James Buchanan's contractarian approach to building upon these foundations, gain significance in this context. These perspectives reveal that the meaning of a constitution goes beyond mere charters drafted in particular historical circumstances. As Tocqueville has made us aware, constitutions are founded on a commitment to a set of political understandings that orient citizens in resolving amongst themselves particular problems of collective action as they may encounter. This notion of problem-solving within institutions that represent such political understandings is explored in the next chapter. These analytical foundations lead us to consider how "good government" can be deliberately constituted.

CHAPTER 7

Adaptive Development and Institutional Problem-Solving

H uman beings continually adapt to their physical and social environment; problem-solving is a constant and core activity (Popper 2001). Every day, individuals encounter problems that they solve singly as well as jointly with others. In both cases, problem-solving proceeds within some explicit or implicit representation of the relevant situation. In cognitive problem solving, our behavior is largely the outcome of the rules and propensities bounded within particular worldviews. In associative problem-solving, our actions and interactions similarly reflect particular representations of the problem environment that we share with others.

Theories of human problem-solving, when applied to problems of social order, can help us understand how constitutional governance can improve the problem-solving capabilities of societies.[1] In this chapter, we examine how human problem-solving is structured and apply this knowledge to the problem of associative problem-solving.

The Structure of Human Problem-Solving

The term *problem-solving* relates to a process by which an organism, through the generation of innovation and through standards of selection, seeks to increase its adaptive fit with respect to predicaments posed by its environment. In evolutionary biology, genetic mutations introduce innovations of possible adaptive utility. The species "solves" the problems posed by its environment through enhanced mating ability, fertility, fecundity, and survivorship of those organisms that possess and/or pass on the helpful trait. Through such introduced innovations, the array of characteristics that we associate with the species change over succeeding generations and, given that the problem environment itself does not change, the system can be said to have shifted to form an adaptive fit (Mayr 1982). The Darwinian system thus deals with a process by which novelty or variation is generated, a process by which innovation is selected based on some "natural" standard, and a process by which such changes are preserved, reproduced, and propagated. In this way, alternatives produced in the features and capacities developed within the system enable an increase in the adaptive fit with respect to solving the problems posed by the environment.

The evolutionary process by which an organism solves the problems posed by its environment operates in the similar manner at all levels of learning and among all organisms. As Karl Popper noted, learning takes place "by the method of trial and error: new relations, new forms, new organs, new modes of behavior, new hypotheses, are tentatively put forward and controlled by error elimination." Such trial and error processes also characterize the "correction and modification of previous knowledge" (Popper 1972). This mode of evolutionary problem-solving at the level of species extends to processes of learning; the same scheme applies equally to the development of new forms among living organisms as to the emergence of new scientific theories. As Popper noted, the growth of knowledge through proposition and elimination of tentative solutions draws from the same critical method from ameba to Einstein.[2] Evolutionary problem-solving applies equally to cognitive and institutional adaptation.

Indeed, any study of adaptation must address itself to the issue of problem-solving. In nonbiological contexts, the study of human problem-solving divides between psychologists, who take up models of cognitive human problem-solving, and social scientists, who study the evolution of culture as resolutions to collective action problems. Herbert Simon and Friedrich Hayek have each raised our awareness of the relatedness of these programs of study. Both have shown how analytical models in cognitive psychology can serve as a foundation for analyzing problems of social order.

As we explore below, Simon's *bounded rationality* and Hayek's *adaptive rationality* explain, in related ways, how our minds work when attempting to solve a problem. Simon considers a relatively fixed framework within which problem-solving takes place. Hayek takes a broader perspective, considering as well how this framework itself is subject to adaptation and change.

Simon's Bounded Rationality

Simon (1986: 362) argues that individuals, given their limited mental ken, attend to only a small part of the complexity around them, basing action on a "highly simplified model of the world." Human rationality is therefore not objectively rational but rather boundedly so.

For an individual confronted with a problem—that is, he or she wants something but does not know immediately what series of actions to perform to get it—the initial step is to form a simple bounded representation of the external environment. Any further resolution of the problem proceeds within the framework of this internal representation. Once represented internally, the system "selects" a particular problem-solving method. When this selected method is then applied, it controls the internal and external behavior of the problem-solver (Newell and Simon 1972).

The application of this particular problem-solving method can be put on hold by triggers set off by more general evaluative processes that monitor this process. When this happens, the cognitive system may try another method within given bounds, reformulate the problem using a new representation, or abandon trying altogether.[3]

While Simon recognizes the broader context within which problem-solving occurs, he concentrates on the mechanics of the process as provisionally bounded. Simon's analysis of human problem-solving relies on testing particular approaches for relevancy without upsetting the overall problem representation. Human problem-solving is represented, metaphorically, as an information processing system (Simon 1995). In turn, Simon defines psychology as the study of the underlying processes that enable people to make decisions, to solve problems and, generally, to think.

Hayek's Adaptive Rationality

Hayek's work complements Simon's contributions to theoretical psychology and extends them to consider more fully the adaptive processes affecting the bounds within which human problem-solving occurs.[4] In *The Sensory Order*, published in 1952, Hayek conceives of the mind as an evolving order that attempts to reflect (though with not perfect success) the salient features of the physical world. The psychologist's task, according to Hayek, is to reconstruct the development of the process by which—or the constraints within which—the organism classifies the physical stimuli encountered in its environment.

According to Hayek (1952a), perceptive predispositions—built up over the course of phylogenetic and ontogenetic development, and manifested in connective neuron fibers—"guide" how we relate to the complexities of the physical world. These predispositions represent conjectured representations of the problem environment and, as such, constitute a semipermanent, imperfect (and perhaps erroneous) "map" of the relations that exist between corresponding physical stimuli. Since impulses recorded by our senses take on perspective when interpreted in the context of these perceptive predispositions, success in recognizing and addressing the problems posed by the environment requires that these maps be subject to continuous reevaluation and adaptive change.

To achieve this, Hayek's poses that our sensory order is structured in terms of layers of nested rules which guide perception, and which are in turn continuously reevaluated for their usefulness in enabling the organism to adapt to its environment. Hayek notes that

> [w]e should have to think of the whole system of connexions as consisting of many vertically superimposed subsystems which in some respects operate independently of each other. Every subsystem of this kind will constitute a partial map of the environment and the maps formed at the lower levels will serve for the guidance for merely a limited range of responses, and at the same time, act as filters or preselectors for impulses sent on to the higher centers, for which in turn, the maps of the lower levels will constitute a part of the environment.[5]

Given this architecture of the sensory order, Hayek (1952a: 113) observes that

> the main significance of any new stimulus will be that it will alter the general disposition for responding in particular ways to further stimuli, and that less and less of its effect will consist in producing a specific response. . . . As we reach higher levels, the classification of impulses becomes thus less specific to a particular function, and more general in the sense that it will help to create a disposition to a certain range of responses to an ever-growing variety of stimuli.

Thus, Hayek (1952a: 115) urges us to conceive of the sensory order as dispositions to interpret stimuli and further, of meta-level dispositions to evaluate and change such dispositions. The apparatus for classification and orientation represents the world in which the organism has existed and, by itself, does not provide full information about the particulars of the current environment. Even as it serves as a semipermanent source of orientation, this structure is itself, in turn, liable to change because of impulses proceeding in it.

The framework of thought is thus self-adaptive or *driven from behind*. It provides, at once, the context for perception, prescription, and action and, at the same time, an evaluation on how well such interpretations permit the organism to solve problems. Learning from experience, the sensory order continuously changes both its structure and its range of operation. The bounds of rationality are, thus, "active" in that while at any given moment the character of decision-making is influenced by the preexisting state of internal processes, these processes are themselves subject to continuous reevaluation and modification.

Inductive and Deductive Problem-Solving

Hayek, thus, draws our attention to the fact that individuals constantly adapt the frameworks within which they grapple with their problem environment. Recent work in cognitive psychology has further elaborated how processes of induction and deduction work in tandem to enable the individual to deal with the problems of the real world. It argues that the structure of knowledge modifies continuously to enable a more adaptive fit.

Although neoclassical economists portray rationality as constrained choice, contemporary psychologists point out that reality constantly tempers the validity of these constraints. That is, selective forces govern the direction of growth of our reasoning framework. If the conclusions of a deductive process do not match reality, then it is possible to revise or clarify their foundational premises. As Stevenson (1993: 65) explains, "human intelligence, as opposed to pure rationality, depends on the ability to tailor the demands of logic to the needs of the real world." While people are inherently logical and cannot help deriving inferences from already known or acquired premises, "in order to make our way in the practical world, we cannot avoid discarding many of these inferences, in favor of others that are inductive in nature. The result of this is that deduction and induction are inextricably linked and cannot be separated in any simple way."

An examination of knowledge modification through the process of problem-solving is basic to the study of induction. The inductive approach poses that individuals pick out patterns considered relevant in some sense and base deductions or predictions on hypotheses so formed.[6] Given that a range of such hypotheses competes for the right to represent the environment, the central problem of induction is one of specifying the *constraints* within which to draw inferences that are pertinent to the problem situation faced. As Holland et al. note, such constraints rest within a higher level of inferential rules; abstract sets of preexisting rules affect our everyday attitudes (Holland et al. 1986).

Viewing induction as being closely tied to problem-solving also "implies that inferences will only be made about representations currently active"—that is, they characterize relevant data from the prevailing environment. When this representation or worldview is no longer valid, permanent change in at least some facet of associated mental models is likely. The trial and error process inherent in evolutionary learning weeds out those representations that no longer provide valid interpretations while generating and strengthening those representations that lead to better prediction. Holland et al. conclude that the inductive mechanism must possess three characteristics: it must evaluate the fitness of existing rules, generate new and possibly useful rules, and, finally, develop (induce) second order "welds" between existing representative models.

Thinking and problem-solving thus proceed at various levels simultaneously. Judgments that require the application of deductive logic to normative principles are thus conceptually distinguished from processes of forming general beliefs in order to organize our knowledge better (Evans 1993). Whereas deductive inferences can only draw out information already implicit in the premises, the commonplace use of inductive inferences to forecast uncertain events is essential for adaptively rational behavior. Inductive inferences may be used to draw out general beliefs which, if found useful, may not necessarily be abandoned in the face of isolated exceptions. This implies that, that which is deductively logical may be irrational with respect to some standard of adaptive behavior and conversely that, that which is illogical may be adaptively rational.

Modern investigations on the relevance of cognitive problem-solving, thus, reinforce Hayek's conception of the complex sensory order as an adaptive framework of rationality.[7] Hayekian adaptive rationality complements and extends Simon's bounded rationality approach by addressing more clearly how those "irrational and non-rational elements that bound the area of rationality"—to use Simon's phrase—are evaluated and modified with respect to their effectiveness in framing the problems posed by complex and dynamic realities.

The Architecture of Human Problem-Solving

Figure 7.1 presents a highly simplified three-tiered schematic representation of the cognitive structure of human problem-solving. Bounded rationality contemplates serial or parallel experimentation with alternative conjectured solutions to the problem (Actions 1, 2, etc.) as bounded within a particular cognitive representation (A) of the problem environment.

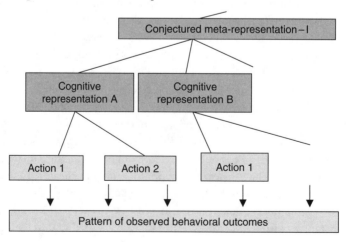

Figure 7.1 The architecture of cognitive problem-solving

Adaptive rationality goes further by considering the overall environment as well. Problem-solving proceeds more broadly within a nested structure of conjectured representations of the problem environment, where alternate cognitive representations compete with each other. Relatively more fixed and general standards based within higher levels of the cognitive infrastructure condition this competition. Repeated failure to develop successful solutions within a particular representation of the problem environment, such as "A," may evoke more reliance on alternatives, such as "B," where this evaluation depends on implicit or explicit terms of competition.

The structure of competition at each level of this structure affects an organism's ability to adapt successfully to its environment. Problem-solving processes working through these routines create an observable pattern of behavior.

The Structure of Institutional Problem-Solving

The Role of Institutions

Institutions facilitate problem-solving by reducing the uncertainties of social interaction. By proscribing some behavioral alternatives and regulating others, the problem-space for collective action is simplified. John R. Commons (1931) defined an institution as "collective action in control, liberation and expansion of human action." He noted that commonly understood rules create a set of common expectations that direct economic behavior. These injunctions, concern "what the individual can, cannot, must, must not, may or may not *do*." Likewise, Douglass C. North (1990) has defined institutions as "the rules of the game of a society, or, more formally, they are the humanly devised constraints that structure human interaction."

Institutions, as complexes of rules socially considered, play an indispensable role in promoting the predictability of our social environment or conversely, reducing uncertainty by confining the scope of activity. In order to be effective as institutions, rules must reduce uncertainty and promote coordination and cooperation among individuals.[8] To fulfill this, institutions have to be, to some extent, *reliable* (triggering consistently under similar circumstances), *recognizable*, (subject to a broad awareness in the community of its characteristics) and *of general applicability* (that is, nonarbitrary or seemingly dependant on general or abstract principles).

Coordinating rules—those enjoining you to drive your car on a particular side of the road, for example—can be self-enforcing since they typically offer little incentive to deviate from the rule. Indeed, driving on the wrong side of the road will likely to result in bent metal and bodily injury—contingencies to which we are normally averse. Solutions to problems of cooperation, in contrast, typically call for meditated rule mechanisms. As the familiar Prisoner's Dilemma story illustrates, there can be a strong motivation in all participants in a cooperative venture to not choose the cooperative strategy for fear of being played the sucker.[9] Here, institutions—by reframing the incentive context of collective action—can help overcome failures of cooperation.

The Origin of Institutions

Institutions, as rule complexes structuring social interaction, can be of spontaneous or pragmatic origin. That is, they can emerge as the unintended result of individual efforts or through the deliberate exercise of common will. Carl Menger's *invisible hand explanation* of the origin of money illustrates how institutional regularities can develop spontaneously. Menger asks, "how can it be that institutions that serve the common welfare and are extremely significant for its development come into being without a common will directed towards establishing them?" Through an exercise in conjectural history, Menger (1984) provides a general theoretical understanding of how institutions could emerge given conditions that could plausibly be considered to have existed. In such an account, given an original situation, individuals try to exploit available opportunities in pursuit of their own interests—developing an abstract unit of exchange to facilitate transactions among themselves, as in Menger's example. If, as is likely at some point, this innovation is discovered to be advantageous, and if others notice this and subsequently imitate such actions, this behavior will become widespread and can result in the social institution to be explained.

While certain types of rules can be expected to emerge from an invisible hand process, others are the outcomes of deliberate processes and, could not plausibly be of spontaneous provenance. In *The Limits of Liberty*, James Buchanan (1975) provides a contractarian account of the emergence of legal order that, like Menger's account, is an exercise in conjectural history.[10] We are asked to imagine an initial condition where each person expends resources to fend off attack by others. Each would be better off if such resources were directed toward production. However, individuals can reduce their investments in warding off predators and go about the business of improving their well-being through collective action once a set of individual rights are defined and accepted. Once individual rights are well-defined, recognized by all participants, and are perceived to be nonarbitrary, realizing value through ordered exchange is possible.

Institutional Evolution Within Adaptive Constraints

The adaptive potential of an institution as a problem solving device—and hence the potential for individuals to adapt to their environment—depends on how well it evaluates and responds to the failures and successes of individuals engaged in collective action. As with adaptive rationality, competition among alternate problem-solving approaches—both *within* particular institutional arrangements as well as *among* institutional arrangements—conditions the character of institutions.

This approach differs from that of standard economic analysis where constraints—budgets, for example—are exogenous to the system. Here, the economic actor is modeled as enhancing his or her well-being within established bounds.[11] The constitutional perspective, by contrast, directs analytical attention to choice among constraints (Buchanan 1996). These may refer to alternative actions circumscribed within the bounds of a given collective choice arrangement or yet may involve some comparison among these collective choice arrangements themselves.[12] Constitutional analysis deals with relative levels of rules and constraints, with the constraints that govern choice at a particular level considered to be a *relatively absolute absolute* (Buchanan 1989a).

Constraints can thus operate at the various nodal points of the structure of institutional problem-solving. They set out the terms evaluating alternative representations of the problem environment or alternative conjectured approaches to solving collective-action problems. Institutional problem-solving, schematized in figure 7.2, is a counterpart to the structure of human problem-solving, depicted in figure 7.1.

Constraints, operating at various nodes of the problem-solving apparatus, include *bounds* on the potential for innovation, *criteria* for selecting from among existing or innovated alternatives, and *restraints* on how to replicate "successes." Bounds, those delineating academic disciplines for example, specify

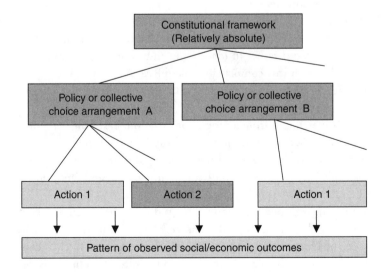

Figure 7.2 The architecture of social problem-solving

adherence to certain core perspectives.[13] Criteria comparing alternative problem-solutions can specify not only what the terms of comparison are but also the way in which the competition is structured. This includes whether the competition is conducted serially or concurrently. The literature on fiscal federalism, for example, highlights the importance of citizen evaluation and choice among competing political jurisdictions. (See, for e.g., Ostrom et al. 1961.) Finally, restraints can play an important role in the spread of successful problem-solving applications. Cultural prohibitions against usury in some early Christian societies, for example, delayed the emergence of important economic institutions in Europe.[14]

Normative Foundations in Crafting Institutional Constraints

Aggregate patterns of social and economic development arise when rational individuals act and interact within institutional constraints. What, however, are the normative bases for evaluating or crafting these constraints? Can we make any claims as to the working properties of alternate rules? In this regard, Viktor Vanberg (1994) makes the important distinction between unconditional and conditional evolutionary claims. He points out that *unconditional evolutionary claims* are statements about which we draw no substantive conclusions as to the desirability of what survives.[15] Alternatively, *conditional evolutionary claims* specify the competitive constraints within which one can make conjecture as to what is likely to be successful and hence survive in an evolutionary process. This distinction focuses attention on the possibility of crafting boundaries, criteria, and restraints for generating, selecting, and propagating institutional innovations for problem-solving.

The scope for crafting institutions as problem-solving devices, thus, rests not so much in debating whether competition among rules or groups will produce efficient outcomes, but rather in identifying and improving the guiding frameworks through which this competition take place. Accordingly, we need to ask what the rules of competition are, and what we can infer about the outcomes of alternative competitive constraints. As Vanberg (1986b) notes, "it cannot simply be postulated that from a process of variation, based on *individual* innovations, and of process of selection, based on *individual* imitation, rules will emerge which benefit the group. Rather, one would have to show *why* and *under what conditions* the process of individual innovation and imitation can be expected to generate socially beneficial rules."

In crafting institutional constraints, how do we choose among alternative values? For the classical liberal, the choice of such a meta-criterion rests in the concept of Normative Individualism. As Vanberg (1994: 189) concludes, "the basic thrust of such a conditional notion of cultural evolution is described by the idea of a process that allows at all levels at which rules and institutions emerge or are chosen, for alternatives to be tried out, and to be exposed to a kind of competition that makes for responsiveness to the interests of the individual persons who live under these rules."

Guided by such normative constraints, the task of a public entrepreneur is to consider and propose adoption of rule constraints conjectured to guide the structure of institutional problem-solving in ways that help develop conditions associated with advanced human development and economic growth.

Implications for Institutional Reform

Institutions as social capital adapt as constituent rules change within an overall framework of problem-solving. Considering institutions as a form of capital, we can see that institutions, like capital, refer to a structure of production. This structure, notes Ludwig Lachmann (1978), assumes a morphology of forms in a nonstationary world. By *structure of production*, Lachmann indicates that complementarity is a central concept in the combined use of capital; by *morphology*, he implies that there are a limited number of such complementarities that are both technically feasible as well as significant; and by *nonstationary*, he introduces the possibility of unexpected change such that it compels a reconfiguration of the structure of capital.

Institutional change similarly depends on the permitted and meaningful complementarities among rules. It is subject also to various contingencies that can arise in a dynamic problem environment. These realities call for caution in implementing institutional change; large-scale reforms may well yield counter-intentional and counterproductive results. As we explore in the following chapter, institutional reform is best initiated from the bottom-up, based on shared understandings, an investigation of prevailing collective-action problems, and a knowledge of prevailing physical, social, cultural, and legal constraints. As we further argue, such institutional adaptation is best facilitated within a system of constitutional governance.

CHAPTER 8

Institutions, Market Exchange, and Development

A s a system of organized exchange, the character of a given market reflects the rules that shape it. Abstract debate framed as to whether "the state" or "the market" is better in promoting development is therefore bound to miss the point. In the real world, the problem-solving potential of any market—and hence its capacity to facilitate development—depends critically on how the context of exchange is structured. These rules of the market are a part of any problem-solving community's common institutional resources. A robust market relies on rules developed and fostered by the governing institutions—whether unofficial or bearing the escutcheon of the state—while the reason for governance, as a facility for problem-solving, is realized through processes of market and nonmarket exchange.

Market or State? Beyond the Ideology

Is the market or state the core dynamic for development? The debate may be more usefully framed to consider how particular market arrangements, as circumscribed variously by the alternative rules can introduce patterns of order we identify with progress. This institutionally robust understanding can help overcome some of limitations commonly identified with market failure and government failure.[1]

Market Failure versus Government Failure as an Issue in Development

Starting with Samuelson (1954) and Bator (1958), the notion of *market failure* has captured the attention of many development economists. Less developed economies, indeed, are often characterized by egregious underproduction of public goods, high transaction costs, and negative externalities—and theories of market failure still provide a cogent theoretical interpretation of these factors (Cowen 1997). Normatively, development theory has drawn on the Samuelson-Bator tradition to propose that the state can play a central role in rectifying conditions of market failure.

Starting from the 1960s, however, and gaining strength through the 1980s, the notion that government intervention could set right perceived market failures was increasingly questioned (Buchanan 1989b). *Government failure*, which took into account rent-seeking behavior among other pathologies of an inefficient public sector, was held out as an equally plausible root of economic backwardness as market failure.[2]

One response to government failure has been to recommend the "privatization" or "marketization" of the economy. This approach, which has often failed to take into account the institutional context of markets, has yielded mixed results in practice.[3] Politically, as well, privatization has been controversial, fed by a widespread perception that privatization prompts greater social iniquity (Alexeev 1999).

The appearance by the mid-1990s of the *Good Governance* program represents another response to the challenge posed by government failure. In promoting Good Governance, the World Bank and other major development agencies acknowledged that "downsizing" state management through privatization of some services is appropriate (World Bank 1997). In this vision, the state was to be further reoriented toward its "core competencies" and "indispensable functions." Foreign aid would help poor countries develop this needed capacity. "The market" may be more efficient, conceded the World Bank, but it is still the unique role of "the state" to care about the poor. The flaw in this approach, developed in chapter 5, is that *Good Governance*—in the sense of an operational strategy—does not diagnose the institutional factors that give rise to the observed characteristics of good governance—in the sense of a desirable state of affairs.

It is clear that market failure as well as government failure occur when information asymmetries and problems of motivation are present. It is also evident that generic markets as commonly idealized do not necessarily present practical solutions to problems of government failure just as state intervention as idealized does not necessarily present practical solutions to fix flawed market processes. This false choice—implied in the debate about the relative superiority of markets or the state as the engine for development—prompts a more careful look at the institutional context of markets and their scope to promote the objectives of development.

Market Institutions and Rule Frameworks

The characteristics we identify with any particular market economy arise from patterns created from a complex of actions and interactions that take place within the rules of this market (Wagner 2002). Specific geographical, legal, and ethical constraints, as well as cultural and language traditions, acting as explicit and implicit constraints, shape the nature of mediated market and nonmarket exchange.

Friedrich Hayek defined an *economy* as consisting "of a complex of activities by which a given set of means is allocated in accordance with a unitary plan among the competing ends according to their relative importance." Hayek (1976: 109) used the term *catallaxy*, by contrast, to refer to a network of relationships that make up a market order. Catallaxy thus captures the idea of "an order brought about by the mutual adjustment of many individual economies in the market. [It is thus] a kind of spontaneous order produced by the market through people acting within the rules of property, tort, and contract."

Rules of the market shape how individuals might use their knowledge of time and place in relation to that of others for their own adaptive benefit. The extent and character of a market order thus depends on how such rules condition the way in which individuals exploit their knowledge through particular processes of exchange. This means that inappropriate or inadequate rules can motivate behavior that, while rational to the individual with respect to extant rule constraints, may spawn failures of cooperation and coordination, with negative implications for development.

The Case of Russia's Privatization

Contemporary Russia illustrates in many ways what happens when appropriate market institutions are absent. With the fall of the Soviet Union, the Russian Federation's transition to an overtly market-based economy involved a massive privatization of formerly state owned industries and other assets (Alexeev 1999; Brainerd 1998). Early Russian reformers considering that political influence over economic life, dominant in the Soviet system, to be the fundamental source of economic inefficiency, believed that Russians would act as "economic men,"—"like the rest of the people in the world"—once the state was no longer interfered in "the natural functioning of the market" (Boychko et al. 1996). They appear to have placed little consideration, therefore, on developing effective limits for types of competitive behavior that could generate a "successful" market order. A "free market"—that is a market where exchange is not made conditional on particular rules—does not, however, necessarily bode well for a well-functioning market. A result is that although Russia has witnessed a significant privatization effort, the lack of effective rules created an environment where harmful institutions, such as the oligarchs and the mafia have emerged.[4]

One outcome is that ruthlessness and sleaze rather than talent and hard work are often the needed ingredients for success in market competition in Russia. As described by *The Economist*, there are in Russia "the natural-resource barons who grabbed the country's oil, gas, and mineral riches after the collapse of communism; there are managers adroit at siphoning off their firm's revenues for personal gain; there are monopolists and cartel-mongers who use their connections to squash competition, and thus make businesses as selling petrol or building materials fantastically lucrative" (*The Economist* 1998). Other palpable outcomes of this neglect of market rules in Russia may include a vexing rise in crime, deepening social inequality, and the development of a significant barter economy.

The Scope for Market-Based Problem-Solving

Market behavior, in the best sense, is motivated by individuals attempting to create value for themselves by seeking to satisfy others through producing something conjectured to be of value to them (A. Smith 2003). Market competition is thus a process of conjectures, trials, and failures or successes in which entrepreneurs try out new products, technologies, services, inputs, modes of production, and advertising, based on estimations of current consumer preferences, and on hypotheses on how best to satisfy them. In turn consumers, through their selective buying decisions provide feedback on what they find appealing. Those entrepreneurs who better anticipate customer needs then have gain a competitive advantage vis-à-vis their rivals.

Rents created by this temporary success motivate the necessary effort and risk-taking of the entrepreneur. The less successful competitors, by losing market share, fall under pressure to improve, by innovating or by imitating those who have been more successful, or to leave the market altogether. As Hayek (1978) points out in *Competition as a Discovery Procedure*, competition is manifested in the rivalry among entrepreneurs who, in seeking to earn profits, learn about consumer preferences while attempting to serve the needs of consumers.[5]

Markets in this way can serve as a facility for problem-solving. After all, entrepreneurs offer for sale various goods and services that they conjecture will solve problems of adaptation that prospective consumers face. For example, an accountant offering to manage your finances or a pharmaceutical vending a new drug hopes to remedy some problem that one may face. Both the accountant and the drug maker hope to improve their own well-being through exchange within a given market structure.

Such market-based problem-solving activities proceed under some (at least implicit) institutional arrangement. The catallactic order that proceeds from within given market rules yield the pattern of social and economic outcomes we observe. Yet, any institutional arrangement is only one among a variety of existing or potential alternatives. This means that in assessing the performance of a system of exchange under prevailing institutional constraints we have the opportunity to consider alternative rules-of-the-market based on an expectation of the working properties of those rules.

Since entrepreneurial creativity, in anticipation of consumer desires, drives competition, the "outcome" of this trial-and-error market process is open-ended rather than predefined. Moreover, the vitality of the competitive process and the character of a market are determined by the rules that govern the ability of that market's participants to innovate, choose, and imitate others' successes. There can exist in a given market, *variation* in the constant emergence of innovation, *selection* through consumer choice, and *duplication*, in the repetition or imitation of strategies, technologies, or products that have been perceived to have led to success. The rules governing the market for civil aviation in India (disussed further) illustrate how rules of the market affect the conduct of entrepreneurial activity, and hence the prospects for adaptive well-being.

The Case of Indian Airlines

The airline industry in India was nationalized and consolidated in 1953 on the premise that a well-rationalized system would provide uniform service across a comprehensive domestic route network.[6] This restructuring was seen to overcome perceived market failures by, among other factors, avoiding equipment redundancies and by providing links to remote locations within India not served by the several small private air services in existence at that time. It granted the state-run Indian Airlines a monopoly over domestic air routes that was to last for forty years.[7]

The rules governing the market for air travel, however, did not serve the needs of the general public well. The rules did not allow competition from alternate air service producers, curtailing plural sources of innovation, error elimination, and learning. Moreover, for Indian Airlines' management, "success" often depended more on the pleasure of government officials than on the satisfaction of the flying public. Thus, while the airline was often considered inefficient from the point of view of the flying public, airlines managers continued to innovate to serve the needs of bureaucrats and politicians. These officials, after all, had control of the airline's budgets, staff assignments, and pay scales and could thus reward and sanction new behavior.

As a result, the officials themselves became the relevant consumers and the airline evolved to serve their needs, rather than that of the public, more effectively. To their chagrin, booked and ticketed passengers on scheduled flights often lost seats, and faced delayed departures (and even changed destinations) to accommodate the travel requirements of important officials.

Problem-solving in the process of evolutionary adaptation is always present. However, as the Indian Airlines case illustrates, such problem-solving should be harnessed through an "appropriate" structuring of the relevant market—such that success in entrepreneurship is rewarded only through identifying and addressing the problem-solving needs of the relevant consumers.

Systems of Rules and Systems of Exchange

Social scientists have, at least since the eighteenth century, been aware of the significance of an appropriate institutional context to foster a desirable market order. Adam Smith, in his *Wealth of Nations*, cited the need for coordinating mechanisms to improve specialization and trade with others. He observed that individuals' activities could only appropriately coordinate under a general legal framework—the "laws of justice"—that established the rules of the game. Such a legal framework would limit competition by excluding the use of coercion, force, fraud, and threats.

In the twentieth century, the German Ordo-Liberal school has stressed the need to design an institutional infrastructure for economic activity (Vanberg 1988). The Ordo view distinguishes the concept of *Wettbewerbsordnung*—the rule of law or institutional framework set to maintain the "proper" functioning of the competitive process—from the concept of *Leistungswettbewerb*—the competitive order of the market that unfolds within such rules.

In making this differentiation, Ordo-Liberals recognized, on one hand, that expectations for the spontaneous formation of a robust economic order within a regime of laissez-faire was overoptimistic, while on the other hand, active intervention by a state to maintain control over economic activity could lead to the loss of liberty.[8] Franz Böhm and Walter Eucken (1952), nucleators of Ordo-Liberalism, laid particular stress on the legal and constitutional preconditions for a liberal market economy. They promoted the concept of *Ordnungspolitik*—literally, the policy toward the organization of the market—as a framework within which to concentrate on how a constitution could provide the guidance within which the market could more efficiently and equitably develop. The involvement of a government in economic affairs rests properly in the formation of an economic order, they held, rather than in ad hoc interventions in the economic process.

If the characteristics of a market order are influenced by the rule structures that circumscribe it, it follows that improvements to a market order must take into account changes in the institutional wellsprings of that order.[9] In turn, this leads us to imagine types of rule innovations that, if introduced, could influence the generation of the sort of outcome patterns that we would consider normatively desirable. Rules embodying such conditional claims specify the competitive constraints conjectured to bring about desired attributes in a market order; as per the Ordo-Liberals, rule-governed processes that restrict competition within particular bounds may be thought to be superior to others if that order which is forecast to be generated by the process so constrained is considered normatively desirable.

Markets and the Scope for Development

In his essay, *The Use of Knowledge in Society*, Hayek (1945) noted that a more complete exploitation by each of his or her "knowledge of time and place" can be realized only through noncentralized institutions of cooperation. Only in this way, Hayek noted, can resources known to members of society best be used for the ends whose relative importance only these individuals know. When entrepreneurs innovate, they attempt to take advantage of their particularized knowledge of available resources, their own capabilities, and their perceptions of needs of others as a way of creating value for themselves. In turn, consumers can improve their well-being through market exchange when their needs are more closely anticipated and problems responded to.[10]

Market competition, if properly structured, can facilitate mutually beneficial exchange, and in this way foster development.[11] Availing market orders can emerge when agreements on certain standards of competitive practice become legitimate within a community of understanding.[12] Such understandings, related variously to codes of ethics, rules of transaction, and units of measurement, help to coordinate necessary transactions within a given market. By subscribing to the institutions that circumscribe market activity, individuals accept limits on the range of possible actions that they may carry out. Such constraints may render the behavior of each participant more predictable to the other, enhancing prospects for successful market-based interactions.

Institutionally robust market rules—including those promulgated by a government—can make possible an increased complexity in the structure of productive capital, which in turn can enable the generation of increasingly sophisticated products and services in anticipation of the problem-solving needs within a market area.[13]

In crafting the rules for such a well-functioning market, we may once again make *conditional evolutionary claims*—that is, we may specify the competitive constraints that we conjecture will enhance mutual well-being through market exchange. As citizens interested in crafting a constitution of development, we are interested in identifying rules of competition that we expect will generate the various dimensions or patterns of order associated with advanced development. One such claim is that a reliable and predictable framework for knowledge-infused market activity rules out ad hoc interventions in the operations in the market. Indeed, piecemeal policy approaches—to correct "market failures" as and when they are seen to occur—limit the scope of the market as a problem-solving device, diminishing the potential for development.

Constituting Market Competition

Drawing together the discussion so far, here are some basic principles of constitutional design for market competition.[14]

First, systems of exchange should be voluntary. However, the conditions under which voluntary exchange takes place need to be specified. Meeting a mugger in a dark alley and confronted with the choice of "your money or your life," most of us would voluntarily hand over our wallets. Appropriately constrained exchange, on the other hand, rules out the use of force, fraud, and threat as legitimate confines for voluntary transaction.

Second, ownership of the means of production, or autonomous limited public ownership of common property resources, should be private. Polycentric problem-solving is vitalized when dispersed proprietorship enables greater use of local knowledge through the functioning of the price system. In addition, if an entrepreneur chooses to organize the resources under his or her purview to offer a good or service in a given market and if this conjecture of needs in that market is not justified, then this initiative is weeded out. By placing his or her own resources at stake, the entrepreneur is more tuned to the problem-solving needs of his or her prospective customers; greater responsibility for economic actions is fostered. As well, such contained failures (in addition to successes) generate information vital to learning inherent in processes of adaptive problem-solving.

Third, market exchange and local public economies should be based on the principle of consumer sovereignty.[15] A basic tenet of Ordo-Liberalism holds that inducing producers to be responsive to consumer interests—by making this the sole channel through which success can be gained—underlies a desirable competitive market order. This prompts the normative determination that the principle of consumer sovereignty should guide the adoption of appropriate evolutionary constraints in a market. As Vanberg and Kerber note, "the claim that markets serve consumer interests is a conditional claim about the working of competition within appropriate rules" (Vanberg and Kerber 1994).

Whereas competition in a Hobbesian anarchy is based on "anything goes," effective limits on the potential range of competitive strategies make a wealth-producing social order possible. Competition among individuals and groups as producers, to serve the interests of other individuals and groups as consumers, within the nexus of the market, as constitutionally constrained, can serve to enhance the adaptive potential of all.

Still, while it may be in the interest of all *as consumers* to live in a society where competition is conditioned on consumer sovereignty, it may be in the interests of each *as producer*, to seek protection in the form of discriminatory treatment from the rigors of competition. As in the case of the Prisoner's Dilemma, a predicament arises where each finds that seeking protection is the dominant choice, making all parties worse-off than they would be in an open competitive environment. Given that it is in the interest of all consumers to live in a competitive market, such an order has to be constitutionally safeguarded against the anticompetitive interests of each as producer. The constitutional framework for a robust market order should accordingly exclude the formation of industrial cartels and other discretionary rules that favor one set of market participants over another. *Fourth, constitutionally conditioned competition has to be complemented by constitutionally safeguarded competition* (Vanberg 1993). A key role of a system of constitutional governance lies in setting up and protecting the competitive system against its given proclivity to decay.

The Market-State Relationship

By recognizing that any market is a spontaneous order circumscribed by institutional bounds, we avoid the quandary of market versus state. *Market failure* arguments fail to account for the variability of institutional settings of the market. They overlook the insight that an adjustment in the rules that frame the market may better deal with its perceived shortcomings than any substituted political mechanism that reallocates the outcome of this process. Arguments for the laissez-faire approach are also carried out in an institutional vacuum, begging the question of what a "true unhampered market" is.

Similarly, privatization without an adequate *Wettbewerbsordnung* will not necessarily succeed in improving the developmental prospects of a society. Merely placing resources in private hands, as in Russia, without specifying conditional claims, places too high and risky a bet that a desirable market order will unfold within some unspecified emergent institutional framework.[16]

A constitutional approach to development emphasizes the tie between the rules for economic and political interaction and development.[17] This chapter and the following one suggest that a political order can be organized along many of the same competitive principles associated with markets, while market orders depend on a constitutional structure based on polycentric principles, to secure the institutional infrastructure for its proper functioning.

PART 3

Crafting Constitutional Governance

CHAPTER 9

Crafting the Institutions for a Problem-Solving Society

How do we bring constitutional governance to practice? In what ways can citizens exercise their creativity to better realize their own well-being along with that of others? What roles do civic entrepreneurs play in this regard, and what promotes and channels their endeavors? This chapter tries to answer these questions in setting out an institutionally robust approach to development.

Polycentric Development

Development is always a *local* phenomenon, where local refers to the relevant problem arena. Human development and economic progress are rooted in the enhanced ability of individuals—brought together within specific contexts and in light of some encountered collective-action problem—to adapt by developing the institutional contexts needed to deal with their situation. To be effective, therefore, institutions must refer to a particular context of a collective-action problem and may ramify to larger domains. Development being necessarily local, it follows that we require a vision of constitutional governance that, while providing overall coherence, is sensitive to the exigencies of time and place. We develop this constitutional vision in terms of the notion of *polycentricity*.

The Meaning of Polycentricity

Michael Polanyi (1951), in *The Logic of Liberty*, describes polycentricity as a process of self-coordination among individuals at and among multiple centers with the actors at each center economizing with respect to his or her present circumstances and constraints. For each such locale, Polanyi stresses the importance of locally relevant, broadly recognized, and non-arbitrary rules. Indigenous problem-solving efforts within the ambit of such rules then contribute to the development of an overall spontaneous order; Polanyi observes that such spontaneous orders come about through numerous mutual adjustments, rather than through deliberate corporate action.

As further refined by Vincent Ostrom (1971), "a polycentric order is defined as one where many elements are capable of making mutual adjustments for ordering relationships with one and other *within a general system of rules* where each element acts with independence of other elements."

The World Wide Web provides a contemporary example of a polycentric order. The Web is composed of groupings where constraining protocols bind individual computer users with similar interests or intents (Ciolek 2003). These protocols are in turn themselves posed within a structure of nested rules and formalities making the ordering of each more or less compatible with those of other groups (Cerf and Kahn 1974). The Web sets the environment within which relevant communities can interact in cyberspace while its own overall form and development is of the nature of a spontaneous order.[1]

Understanding polycentricity directs us to consider its relevance to institutional design: How can we foster desirable patterns of development through attention to the nature of institutional arrangements within a polycentric context? Polycentricity helps us conceive how to strike a balance between processes of adaptation at the local level within specific institutional artifacts and a need for overall coherence within a system of human relationships.

Polanyi's polycentricity as a principle of social organization reflects Hayek's insight that centralized supervision of the economy is impracticable since it is impossible to collect the knowledge of time and place reposed among disparate individuals (and that even if the relevant data were available, the task of assimilating this would be excessive (Hayek 1945). It also enlarges the scope for self-coordination than that often seen in centrally directed systems of governance, although the extent to which a polycentric system can develop is governed by the institutions of property and exchange.[2]

Polycentric governance refers, correspondingly, to the existence of overlapping arenas of political authority. These arenas are present at various scales from local community organizations to national governments and international organizations. Within a polycentric conception of governance, local political units have greater discretion to solve local problems; access to local epistemological resources enhances this discretionary ability. (Residents of a particular area are more likely to possess knowledge about, for example, local soil and weather conditions, and local institutional arrangements.) Effective problem-solving relies crucially in incorporating such local wisdom.[3]

Polycentricity as a principle of constitutional design further requires that local exercise of discretion be constrained both *within* a political unit as well as *among* political units. In the polycentric conception, sovereignty is vested in citizens who, through processes of engagement within diverse though linked, institutional contexts, struggle to find solutions to their own common challenges and, in this way, strive to realize their shared hopes. Limits to the exercise of power with others is invoked both within a political unit—in terms of setting up the appropriate conditions of competitive engagement among alternative policy or action alternatives—as well as among them. Polycentric governance based on fostering local problem-solving competencies through motivating civic participation. Since all authority is to be subject to limits such that no single entity can exercise complete discretion, a polycentric system of government more keenly activates Montesquieu's 1748 precept of using power to check power.[4]

Polycentricity and Institutional Problem-Solving

Systems of constitutional governance based on polycentric design principles differ from those of unitary state governance in their relative emphasis on systemic checks and balances. In the ideal, unitary forms can serve as institutional problem-solving devices. In practice, however, their structure can limit the capacity of a system of state governance to learn and adapt. It is also true that while the ideal polycentric systems of governance enable individuals to learn and adapt within facilitative structures for collective problem-solving, these organizations in practical terms are, in and of themselves, not inherently effective. Rather, it is the nature and application of constraints within a polycentric organization that brings out its problem-solving potentials.

As noted in the previous chapter, the institutional problem-solving approach sets out how alternative conjectured approaches to solving problems of collective action are admitted and weighed within some overall "meta" constitutional standard. In this regard, the effectiveness of a polycentric constitutional framework as an adaptive system depends variously on processes of innovation, trial, and evaluation among alternative policies and actions. Two factors affect the pattern of social and economic developmental outcomes within any constitutional context: the first has to do with the *availability* of alternative problem-solving approaches. The second concerns the *assessment* of these alternatives.

These two factors are strongly complementary. The idea of constitutional governance based on polycentric design offers the potential for more effective governance, where each among multiple contexts of governance could be tuned better to the relevant collective-action problem faced by the particular collectivity.

To this, the institutional problem-solving perspective emphasizes the role of conditioning rules, encouraging us to consider constitutional governance in a more dynamic context of trial, evaluation, and replication or change. It urges us to flesh out the rule context within which constitutional governance can be effective.

Polycentricity, while necessary for constitutional governance, is in itself an insufficient condition for facilitating development. While a local administration can facilitate the use of local knowledge and make participation in forums of collective choice easier, the gains associated with these tangible components are by no means guaranteed without the presence of a complementary (if often directly imperceptible) institutional framework which conditions the process through active competitive constraints.

Polycentric Governance Within Adaptive Constraints

Polycentricity is often confused with decentralization since, in the broadest of terms, they both refer to a dispersal of the authority and administrative functions to regional or local levels.[5] The term "decentralization" is commonly interpreted to include *political devolution* where constitutional provisions grant greater discretionary authority to regional governments over policy, and *administrative deconcentration* where greater discretion to carry out policy objectives is provided to regional governments (Felser 1982). Although seemingly involved with constitutional governance, decentralization, as commonly conceived, often lacks institutional depth in that it frequently fails to take into account the nature and placement of constraints with a system of government.

Depending on the prevailing institutional circumstance, proposals to devolve and deconcentrate the exercise of governance will either succeed or fail to improve development (Olowu 1999). Indeed, results of real world attempts at decentralization are mixed. Interpreting this evidence, proponents and skeptics of more diffusely structured governance have argued over the merits and limits of decentralization, generating much heat but little light.[6] Indeed, it is quite possible to find a contradictory example for every positive experience with decentralization.[7] Yet, the point often lost in such discussions is the need to elaborate an institutional bracing to support development through a polycentric design of governance.[8]

In contrast to decentralized state governance, constitutional governance refers not only to the dispersal of the authority to local communities to make decisions and implement them—as per polycentric principles—but to the conditioning mechanisms that make these institutional innovations workable and sustainable as well. While decentralization, as usually understood, is a top-down process of reallocating the authority to problem-solve, polycentricity, by contrast, focuses upon bottom-up processes of problem-solving where citizens involve each other in policy experiments.

Political units typically form around sets of commonly faced collective-action problems. Village level or other provincial polities tend to coalesce about parochial issues concerning the management of public goods and common-pool resources—whether physical (such as a water source) or institutional (rules governing rights to property and exchange, for example). Once they form, the local institutional capacity has to advance to deal with matters of potential conflict and cooperation in the civic life of the community.

In turn, institution-strengthening within the framework of polycentric governance directs analytical scrutiny first on the constitutions of these local institutional problem-solving devices and next upon the context within which each of these local units may relate to each other. Within the constitutional context of a particular problem-solving unit, the institutional problem-solving framework guides us to consider how to structure and weigh (through processes of collective decision-making) alternative approaches to commonly perceived problems. Analytically, such venues for decision-making exist at the choice nodes of the institutional problem-solving framework.

If we take up a particular problem as a reference point for analysis and see what institutions have arisen to manage it, we can begin to examine how competition shapes its institutional capacity. We can look first at the how alternative rules are proposed, compared, and chosen *within* that unit, and next examine in what ways individuals can compare and choose *among* alternative rule systems.

Within our regime of reference, given rules and regulative structures set out permitted or proscribed activities. These importantly include constraints on how individuals are to compare alternative mooted solutions—policy options, if you will—to problems of collective action. As such, institutional construction and reconstruction requires that we deal with fundamental constitutional issues: Who sets the agenda? What are the *limits* on proposing new rules or institutional innovations? What are the processes for comment and contribution? What are the *criteria* for selecting among these? Who has standing? How do we reach collective agreement? How do we restrain majorities from exercising tyranny? How do we invoke "checks and balances" to constrain this tendency? What *restraints* exist in replicating routines that have proved successful in one sphere of problem-solving to another? What processes weed out poorly performing institutional sub-routines? How do we make such judgments collectively? How frequently do we make them and so on.

Among our chosen units of public choice, we can again ask ourselves what the competitive constraints are. How are we to evaluate and modify the formats for day-to-day policy judgments? How do we compare the rules and regulatory structures of one unit with that of another? For example, are individuals able to express preferences among rule-making units by voting with their feet or their check-books? How can agents of government deputed to make social choices and administer solutions to problems of collective action be constrained?[9]

Competition, when conditioned among problem-solving approaches within particular institutional arrangements as well as among these institutional arrangements themselves, can lead to institutional vibrancy. Past events, choices, and the accepted institutional routines—as exist variously at local, collective, and constitutional choice levels—help establish the particular contexts for problem-solving. More fully conceived, the process of development is then one of elaborating or modifying present institutional structures through refining presiding constraints to improve the problem-solving capacity of citizens in their given or chosen community.

Reconciling Institutional Coherence with Adaptive Change

The competence of systems of collective action, as instruments tuned to collective problem-solving, depend on the elaboration and conditioning of their structure. The approach here stands in contrast to the abstraction of the state as a benign agent devoted to promote human development and economic progress. State governance, in its ideal form, takes up these tasks through the expert preparation and professional administration of policy prescriptions. The monocentric structure and neglect of constraints implied in this framework for state governance strongly diminish the problem-solving capabilities of many developing societies.[10] It is ironic that the application of the framework of state governance to the theory of development has the potential to worsen the practical objectives of economic growth and human development.

Viewed from the vantage of a ruler, polycentricity is untidy and confusing: whereas the postwar development framework places economic analysis and policy development within a clear theoretical framework with which many of today's theoreticians and practitioners are at ease, the constitutional governance perspective takes into account myriad institutional settings and encourages local experimentation with alternate rule structures. Policy development and its administration are no longer distinct aspects of a science of development.

Yet, while the postwar state-based development framework lends itself to coherence in policy analysis, constitutional governance seeks coherence in institutions within which citizens as civic entrepreneurs, each acting within his or her own context, can take initiative to overcome problems of collective action to enhance their own well-being and that of others. State governance provides coherence from the point of view of the ruler whereas constitutional governance provides coherence from the point of view of the citizen.

Civic Entrepreneurship in Problem-Solving

In considering systems of collective action as a problem-solving device, we have hitherto occupied ourselves with the structure, form, and role of institutions. We now turn to the constitutional dynamics of institutional problem-solving—that is, we examine *how* these institutional structures evolve, *who* develops them, *why* and *when* such changes are prone to occur, and within *what* constraints.

Any observed pattern of developmental order is the result of individuals acting and interacting within a complex structure of rules and conditioning constraints, where this framework itself is subject to evolutionary change. As we noted in chapter 3, this change can be analyzed at three levels (E. Ostrom 1999).

At the immediate or *action level* are particular approaches to an observed problem situation. These approaches correspond with existing or potential solutions to the collective-action problem as conceived. This intermediate or *collective choice level*, thus, represents a particular way of representing the problem environment. It sets the terms of reference for particular solutions and, as well, sets the terms within which these solutions can be compared. Finally, the *constitutional level* sets out the terms within which to condition and compare alternative institutional arrangements—as exists or is imaginable. Each of these levels is relatively more fixed with respect to the alternatives they frame; they serve as provisionally given points of coordination within which institutionally coherent innovation at a particular level can proceed.

The approach of institutional problem-solving, developed earlier, sets out how adaptation can take place within each of these different levels of constraints. It helps us understand how alternatives, introduced among conjectured problem-solving approaches, could be assessed, and how institutions can evolve as a result. This perspective makes clear that the adaptive success of citizens engaged in processes of collective action depends not only on the nature of institutional constraints framing problem-solving within and among given arenas, but also on how citizens introduce new rules as putative solutions within this framework.

The challenge of developing with others the rules needed to manage more tangible problems of collective action is, in itself, a problem of collective action.[11] In expanding on this point, we first take up the role of the entrepreneurship in the evolution of institutions. Following this, we consider the constraints that shape it. After taking these steps, we can begin to see the relevance of sensitive institutional design to social and economic development.

The Nature of Civic Entrepreneurship

The role of entrepreneurs, in introducing creative and unique solutions to problems of collective action, is critical to governance. The nature and role of these civic entrepreneurs, thus, requires elaboration. We identify the characteristics and motivations of public entrepreneurs first (answering the *who* and *why* queries noted earlier) before addressing the contexts (*when* and *where*) within which they operate.

A civic or public entrepreneur is one who fosters the process of institutional problem-solving by posing alternatives to current ways of dealing with issues of collective action.[12] He or she compares established problem-solving arrangements with other imagined or available alternatives. Such initiatives appear in the context of proposed or optional conjectured approaches to solving a given dilemma of collective action with respect to some reigning institutional arrangement, or of alternatives to the conjectured institutional arrangement itself within a broader constitutional context. As such, a public entrepreneur seeks to address the problem as understood by looking outside the confines of the issue as nominally defined. Yet, public entrepreneurs need not be "angels." They too expect to be rewarded for their efforts with tangible and intangible rewards. And their efforts at innovation have to be conditioned within broader normative constraints.

Not unlike their market counterparts, civic or public entrepreneurs first recognize a problem and its context, then envision a remedy through a reevaluation of that context, and finally initiate and manage the transition to the new problem-solving regime.[13] As such, they bear some resemblance to Joseph Schumpeter's notion of a business entrepreneur. Indeed, within Schumpeter's theory of economic development, change produced endogenously by pioneering entrepreneurs leads to a perennial gale of restructuring and expansion.

According to Schumpeter (1947: 152), entrepreneurship is neither an occupation nor a profession but a rarely found capacity for "innovation," which he describes as the carrying out of new combinations of resources. Such entrepreneurial activities give rise to an incessant competitive restructuring of the economy. The personality and motivation of the entrepreneur predicates economic change. As such, it is not as much in the creation of new ideas as it is in their implementation that the essence of Schumpeter's entrepreneur is found; as Schumpeter notes, "the inventor produces ideas, the entrepreneur 'gets things done' . . . It is in most cases only one man or a few men who see a new possibility and are able to cope with the resistances and difficulties which action always meets with outside the ruts of established practice."

Thus, to use an expression popular in business school circles, an entrepreneur "thinks outside the box." He or she stands in contrast to a "static administrator" who economizes within the bounds of a posed problem or worldview (Schumpeter 1911). An entrepreneur solves problems inductively while the static administrator is limited to doing so only deductively.

While business entrepreneurship refers to new or unconventional ways of combining resources to meet the imagined need of consumers within given rules of market exchange, civic entrepreneurship deals with refreshing the rules and institutional bounds within which collectivities jointly solve their common problems.[14] Against this understanding, we draw, as per Vincent Ostrom, the distinction between *culture* and *politics*. Ostrom (1997: 203) defines culture as "a *configuration of relationships* that brings together ideas and deeds with places inhabited and cultivated by people, and kept in good repair through assorted activities of cultivating, building, instituting, and doing what it is that people seek to achieve." In turn, politics "is concerned with pooling, rearranging, compromising existing interests while *creating and maintaining the working arrangements*" of units of governance—from, variously, that of the household to the nation—within some normative constraints in pursuit of achieving greater adaptive potentials.

What motivates the public entrepreneur? Why might we expect to see exertions in civic entrepreneurship?

If economists regard agents as impelled by the urge to maximize utility, political scientists are wont to explain issues of motivation by invoking the concept of power.[15] In the political science literature, the notion of power as a motivator originates with Hobbes who noted *Leviathan* in "a general inclination of all mankind, a perpetual and restless desire for power after power, that ceaseth only in death." Power, as traditionally interpreted, involves exercising *power over* others through privileges in rule making and control over resource allocations. Harold Lasswell, notably, associated power with the command and control of the instruments of coercion. In systems of state governance, power relates to gaining access to positions of authority within a legally determined hierarchy (Lasswell and Kaplan 1950).

By contrast, the concept of *power with*, as emphasized by Vincent Ostrom (1997), gains relevance in discussions of polycentric governance. Referring to Hobbes' observation that "the POWER *of a man*, to state it universally, is his present means, to obtain some future apparent good," Ostrom interprets that the motivational force rests in "taking actions in arranging present means in appropriate ways to realize future apparent goods." The task of arranging present means to deal successfully with an uncertain world requires a suitable framework of rule-ordered relationships.

Given that problem-solving takes place within a particular cultural (qua institutional) framework, a science of association has then to refer to innovations in constitutional design to improve prospects of overcoming obstacles in the realization of future apparent goods. The task of the public entrepreneur is then to visualize and to innovate changes to the cultural and legal constitution of a collectivity as a way of potentially enhancing the prospects, for each, of developing their *power with* others. The public entrepreneur augments, in association with members of his or her community, common institutional resources to enhance mutual prospects for future well-being—as within the context of a prevailing constitutional framework.[16]

Constitutional Adaptation Within Adaptive Constraints

Public entrepreneurs serve an important civic role in proposing alternative institutional arrangements. The contexts where these are proposed and debated are equally significant. We, thus, turn now to *where* and *when* changes in the constitutive rule framework take place.

Implicit in rules are certain hypotheses about future patterns of action and interaction that come about by individuals abiding by the rules. When these claims about the working properties of a rule are unconditional, we cannot draw substantive conclusions as to the desirability of what patterns emerge. By contrast, conditional claims specify selective commitments and constraints based on what we expect will emerge or survive through the workings of particular rules or conditions (Vanberg 1994: 184). Constitutions, as social covenants, should reflect conditional conjectures in committing and constraining subsidiary rules in how they may be proposed and adopted. Constitutional level rules set out the criteria by which sub-constitutional decisions may be made as well as establish the conditions under which competition among sub-constitutional rules may be played out.

The presence of a constitutional framework that conditions the introduction of institutional innovation through restricted forms of public entrepreneurship presumes certain normative evaluations regarding the changing rule order. Such a conditioning framework limits the introduction of institutional innovation to prescribed forums (particular amendment procedures or petition requirements, for example) and sets standards by which civic debate among presented options proceed.

The presence of a conditioning constitutional framework also allows us to deal with two incentive-related difficulties that arise with public entrepreneurship in institutional problem-solving. In the first instance, these relate to *strategic motivations* in processes of rule renegotiation. In the second, they relate to *information asymmetries* related to interests and theories about the working properties of rules. Let us deal with them in turn.

Experimentation among rules with selection based on full unanimity can be cumbersome, particularly in large groups. Unanimity signifies a higher level of legitimacy because of the voluntary nature of the rule adoption and because it indicates the development of a community of understanding through the acknowledgement of each of the rules now in play. However, strict unanimity as a criterion in the adoption of rule change can lead to strategic *hold-out*. Here, each interested party is motivated to withhold consent to the mooted institutional innovation in order to realize his or her best strategic position (Brennan and Buchanan 1985).

Further, personal sacrifice, if needed to champion change, can inhibit public entrepreneurship. Such public spiritedness is inhibited when expected benefits, gained by securing power with others, fails to offset personal costs for developing rule innovations. Considerations of *publicness* can consequently paralyze institutional transformations needed to deal with changes in the nature of collective action problems (Ibid.).

These issues bring to attention the importance of the incentive contexts within which alternatives in public entrepreneurship are encouraged, gauged, and adopted. Sensitivity to the contexts of constitutional choice can help relieve some of these problems of motivation.

In negotiating particular constitutive rules, individuals may also hold theories about the working properties of alternative rules as well as bear interests based on the subjective evaluations of their expected outcomes (Buchanan and Vanberg 1989). Given these *interests and theories*, as well as levels of engagement in the rule-making process, individuals involved in constitutional negotiations face incentives to introduce biased rules. Given that these rules initiate how subsequent rule-making is to take place, there exists in the negotiation of rules at the constitutional level potential for a greater impulse to be fair. When rules at the constitutional level are more abstract, rule-makers may not be able to anticipate accurately the particular ways in which they may be confronted in the future by their own rules. As a result of this *veil of uncertainty*, rule entrepreneurs face a greater inclination to be fair.

Indeed, the more general the constitution level rules are and the longer the period over which they are to apply, the less certain individuals will be about how proposed rules will affect them. As such, rules at the constitutional level should reflect more abstract principles than rules at sub-constitutional levels. Such constitutional principles as developed can, in turn, forestall the introduction of rules that differentially benefit one party or another.

Constitutional level rule-making can also relieve the hold-out problem associated with the unanimity criterion for social consent for decision-making at the collective choice (or policy) level. In considering the potential for strategic behavior, paralysis, and the practical difficulties in seeking even near unanimity acceptance for everyday collective decision-making, we can follow, as noted earlier, the wisdom of James Madison in shifting unanimity approval for rule changes at the constitutional level and adopt various margins of majority voting for lower levels of rule experimentation in problem-solving.

Rule making at the level of collective choice, such as those generated by legislatures or local councils, derive their legitimacy through the larger constitutional agreement. In this way, collective choice rule-making allow for rules to be provisionally tried-out and evaluated. In this regard, Buchanan (1960) notes that majority rule

> provides the opportunity for any social decision to be altered or reversed at any time by a new and temporary majority grouping. In this way, majority decision making itself becomes a means through which the whole group ultimately gains consensus, that is, makes a genuine social choice. It serves to insure that competing alternatives may be experimentally and provisionally adopted, tested, and replaced by new compromise alternatives approved by a majority group of ever-changing composition.

A constitutional framework of a system of collective action, as a conditional evolutionary claim for the development of beneficial rule structures or institutions, can lower the threshold of publicness and thus improves the problem-solving potential of society. It can help provide the conditions for collective action that we conjecture to be well-adapted to problem-solving and development.

In accepting that polycentric forms lend themselves to superior efforts in institutional problem-solving, we have emphasized the centrality of local forums for public decision-making. This focus lowers the threshold of effort in public entrepreneurship; or in other words, public entrepreneurship as a means to gain *power* with others can regain relevance as a motivating factor for institutional reinvigoration, and consequently development, in systems of polycentric governance.

Some Principles of Constitutional Design

The constitutional constraints framing systems of collective action are crucial to their capacity as problem-solving devices. Four principles of constitutional constraints can be summarized, based on the preceding analysis.

First, competition among pubic entrepreneurs should be organized within constitutionally legitimated venues. Adoptions of new systems of rules would have to pass through relevant procedures of promulgation (such as amendment, petition, consensus, etc.) as set out. Normatively, the use of force and threat (such as in military coups) would be ruled out as a sanctioned form of public entrepreneurship.

Large scale political events such as war and political unrest, geological events such as floods or earthquakes, or severe economic conditions, such as depressions, each of which touch the lives of large numbers of people, often act to form a widespread consensus for some manner of constitutional change. They help develop a community of understanding, often providing the focus needed for public discussion engaged on constitutional alternatives. As Madison noted in *Federalist 49* with respect to the American revolutionary experience,

> We are to recollect that all existing constitutions were formed in the midst of danger which repressed the passions most unfriendly to order and concord; of an enthusiastic confidence of people in their patriotic leaders, which stifled ordinary diversity of opinions on great national questions; of a universal ardor for new and opposite forms produced by universal resentment and indignation against the ancient government; and whilst no spirit of party connected to the changes to be made or abuses to be reformed, could mingle its leaven in the operation.

Political revolutions, such as the one alluded to above, arise when venues for institutional change enabling local problem-solving efforts to deal with local exigencies are blocked within the prevailing constitutional order. Revolutionary changes in constitutional paradigms—brought about when motivated segments of the population are willing to experiment with constitutional alternatives—tend to be unconstrained processes, not necessarily subject to specific normative conditioning criteria. Recall, in this regard, the divergent outcomes on the heels of political revolutions in America and France in the eighteenth century as a call for caution.

Second, rule experimentation within an overall constitutional framework should be introduced at the level of the problem situation so as to incorporate local knowledge more fully. Polycentric forms of governance, we have seen, constrain the realm of collective choice and collective action while emphasizing the utilization of local knowledge. We make the conditional evolutionary claim that such constraints enhance prospects for human and economic development through improving the capacity for solving problems of collective action.

Polycentric governance enhances development since it accommodates parallel, institutional experimentation. It allows for alternative rule structures and solutions to collective-action problems to be tried out in different jurisdictions as may be appropriate given the particular cultural habits and geographical idiosyncrasies of each locale. Local experimentation encourages public entrepreneurship by making more palpable the expected benefits of seeking power *with* others and by lowering the individual effort needed in this respect. It also develops knowledge through creating natural experiments for studying the relationship between particular complexes of rules and resulting patterns of social order in each of many community governments. In addition, citizens with a polycentric system of governance, have the potential to identify and choose desirable packages of institutional features associated with particular jurisdiction, and to locate themselves accordingly at lower cost.

Third, individuals or groups that manage to obtain some benefits from their own initiative should be able to enjoy the benefits of that action, as long as their doing so does not impose unreasonable costs on other members of that society. Public entrepreneurship should be constrained through conditioning constitutional rules in such a way that rule innovators are not motivated by rewards that benefit a particular constituency to the detriment of the interests of others (Vanberg and Kerber 1994). We expect constitutional systems that channel public entrepreneurship through centralized mechanisms of rule change to be less adept in constraining public entrepreneurship in this regard.

Indeed, centralized governance, especially in larger polities, implies that the locus of public decision-making is remote from the arena of collective action. As rule-making becomes more inaccessible and opaque, watchfulness over this process becomes more challenging, and opportunities increase for entrepreneurial activity that benefits one group at the expense of others. Often, legislation that fosters such distributional consequences is deceptively worded so as to appear to be in the public interest. As the authority to effect and administer rule changes becomes more concentrated, such positions come to reflect a *power over* others. Such command and control over the instruments of coercion—justified as a means to rationalized public policy—can create attendant to it, the various pathologies associated with rent seeking and corruption.

Finally, constitutional design should limit the scope for particular groups to take over rule-making prerogatives. Tocqueville (2000) addressed this point in his analysis of American governance in the early to mid-nineteenth century. He noted that although the United States was constituted on principles of federalism, this was not always true of the governments of the states. Given that state constitutions at that time provided for few checks on the tyranny of the majority, Tocqueville foresaw that majority coalitions would soon dominate the legislative, executive, and judiciary branches of government. He predicted that this would undermine constitutional governance and replace it with state governance.

Indeed, innovations in state and local politics in the United States, wherein candidates for the executive, legislative, and judicial branches of government run as a part of a state, led, by the late part of the nineteenth century, to the domination of processes of public decision-making by party bosses who functioned as monopolists, controlling government decisions by integrating command of the legislative, executive, as well as judicial branches of government (V. Ostrom 1971). Instruments of governance became the means by which political power brokers enhanced their influence and wealth rather than a means to solve collective action-problems.

*   *   *

In moving toward a problem-solving society, constitutional governance must refer not only to the dispersal of authority but also to the nature, place, and structure of institutional constraints if it is to be both workable and sustainable. The principles of constitutional design summarized above can provide some normative guidance for the development of a liberal constitutional order. The issue of how to reconcile each of the inevitable multiple, and potentially contradictory and overlapping, localized problem-solving initiatives within a broader political economy is key to polycentric development. They concern how individuals can craft the rules of association with which to solve practical problems without necessary recourse to "the state" as idealized or to "the market" as idealized.

CHAPTER 10

Crafting New Institutions on Indigenous Foundations

I n moving from theory to practice, where can we begin? Crafting capabilities for self-governance begins by acknowledging prevailing institutions that actually guide how individuals associate with each other in various local contexts.[1] Even though these institutions, as inherited, may not be optimal solutions to current collective-action problems, they are valuable as a shared point of orientation for individuals in a community. The challenge of constituting development involves drawing out and building on these existing institutional resources to meet new challenges of collective action (Shivakumar 2003).

The experience of pastoralists in Somaliland, who have adapted their traditional ways of covenanting to build the institutions needed to address contemporary challenges, illustrates how we can move from theory to practice. These pastoralists have not only crafted institutions governing water reservoirs and grazing grounds, but have also constituted more abstract common-pool resources such as local and regional governments. As the case study in this chapter shows, these feats are made more remarkable given the physical and institutional destruction caused by civil conflict leading up to and following the collapse of the state of Somalia.

Discovering Indigenous Capacities

Indigenous institutions are crucial points of reference in conflict resolution and development because they represent current understandings, whether tacit or explicit, among a local population. These understandings often concern how individuals relate to each other with respect to shared problems of collective action. In this way, the term "indigenous institutions" more accurately reflects "locally focused" rather than "traditional" facilities for problem-solving. Crafting meaningful new institutions for self-governance involves drawing on both local communities of understanding and on local knowledge.

Drawing on Communities of Understanding

Indigenous traditions as variously evolved or constituted represent an institutional framework for collective action. Collective action is facilitated when members of a group share certain perspectives—or constitute a community of understanding—about their common problem situation. Shared or commonly bounded ways of looking at the problem environment make the behavior of the one more intelligible to the other, facilitating coordination and cooperation needed to solve collective-action problems.

Language further links these communities of understanding through the articulation of shared concepts. As Vincent Ostrom (1997: 136) points out, "since human beings are unable to read each other's minds directly, the task of developing a method for ordering behavior in relation to one another requires recourse to language. Language now becomes the basis for stipulating rules, so that disparate individuals can act with expectations that others will behave in accordance with those rules." Indeed, the very fact that two individuals communicate through a common language discloses that they concur to a significant degree on the use and manner of relating crucial concepts; after all, even if they disagree, they are in common awareness of the point in contention.

The importance of a commonality in perspective to solving problems of collective action implies that new institutional arrangements must be crafted on a foundation of shared understandings. New concepts have to be articulated using existing vocabulary that refers to currently shared representations. New communities of understanding underlying new institutions for collective action, likewise, have to be crafted through drawing out and modifying existing shared concepts.

Capturing Local Knowledge

The importance placed on locally focused institutions contrasts with the view that a science of development can be drawn from a universal rationality common to all humans and cultures. In this neoclassical view, it is possible to draw out basic postulates and underlying social and economic regularities, leading to the prediction and control of social phenomena at large.[2] Accordingly, problem-solving is relegated to experts who, in applying statistical facts to a general theory, seek to implement their policy determinations upon the society as a whole.[3]

Such centralized approaches to solving problems of collective action however include little of the knowledge of time and place that individuals possess about their own particular circumstances. This knowledge includes fundamental understandings that individuals possess about the character of their physical surroundings and the nature of exchange relationships gained through their unique life experiences (Brennan and Buchanan 1985).

In his essay, *The Use of Knowledge in Society*, Friedrich Hayek (1945) notes that a more complete exploitation of the "knowledge of time and space," where each individual has a specialized understanding of his or her particular circumstances as superior to others, can be realized only through noncentralized institutions of cooperation. Correspondingly, the problem of utilizing the knowledge in society then becomes one of how to develop and modify prevailing rules and constitutional amenities such as to harness more effectively the problem-solving potentials latent in various locally focused indigenous institutions.

Starting from Here

Given that indigenous institutions represent the grammar-in-use of human action and interaction within any particular problem-solving community, we have to take them as our point of orientation in considering initiatives to improve patterns of social and developmental outcomes.[4] Any reordering of the elements of social capital has to take account of the basic cognition held by each within an existing community of understanding.

This need for members of a problem-solving community to come to a new understanding and to adopt new routines and expectations therefore serves as a constraint on the scope and pace of adaptive evolution of social capital.

We next describe the experience of Somali pastoralists in "starting from here." Their experience in drawing on indigenous institutions to craft new institutions to rebuild and maintain common pool resources following a devastating civil war illustrates the practical potential of the constitutional perspective on development.

Constituting Somaliland

The harshness of the physical landscape has helped to shape key indigenous institutions of the people of the northern Horn of Africa.[5] The land is largely scrub desert with brush vegetation supporting the grazing of livestock—the main economic activity. Rain in most areas is severely limited in terms of both measurement and frequency. These conditions place stress upon available underground water sources and land for grazing.

This terrain supports Somali pastoralists who are organized within nomadic clan groups. This clan social structure, as the anthropologist I.M. Lewis (1961, 1994) points out, has evolved to enable the survival of these pastoralists in their harsh environment. Ranging far and wide, alone with their herds of camels and flock, Somali pastoralists are fiercely independent and rely on their own resourcefulness for survival. As nomads, these Somalis have no tradition in centralized government. Rather, they derive their identity from their clan association, a patrilineal system where each member can trace their lineage to a founding father. As we see in the following paragraphs—, clan identity—a key institution—provides for the security of its members as well as collectively enforces the relevant property rights of its members.

Identifying Indigenous Institutions

Clans are broken into units as based on the *dia*, or blood compensation system. The compensation for taking a man's life is one hundred camels and the compensation for taking a woman's life is fifty camels. Individual social units are accordingly based on the security formed through pooling enough livestock so as to form a *dia*-paying group (as this in effect forms a credible threat to take the life of a member of another clan).

The members of a *dia* group are also pledged to support each other in collective political and jural responsibility. For example, the property of the members of one clan is secured against seizure by those of other clans through threats of retaliation by the entire group. Decisions within the group are made by a council of clan elders, who are the heads of families and other respected figures. Rules for self-governance within these units are adopted based on a unanimous consensus. It is in this respect that Lewis refers to the Somali system of governance as a pastoral democracy.

Xeer, representing a tradition of ad hoc covenants, govern relations among members of different clan units, particularly with respect to the sharing of common-pool resources such as grazing land and water sources. There are typically strong sanctions for violating these *xeer* with monitoring and enforcement controlled by the *Guurti* or inter-clan Council of Elders. These *xeer* are developed as and when they are needed to cope with the presence in the proximate rangeland of other nomadic *dia* groups. Even so, conflict has always been the leitmotif of interclan relations as the temptation to raid the other group's cattle is always present while monitoring such behavior is very difficult.

The *dia* offers security to the Somali pastoralist through the threat of collective retribution while the *xeer* provides a traditional form of compacting among clan units as they may encounter each other. As evolved, these indigenous institutions have proved to be of adaptive use to the nomadic pastoralist.

They accommodate the need for independent decision-making by the pastoralist on the range and set out the formalities through which cooperation between particular units can be developed as and when needed. As required for a nomadic population, these institutions, as based on agnatic kinship, transport well.

On the other hand, such systems of collective action have tended to fare poorly when sustained cooperation among different clan units is required. Retaliation for minor torts—based on a tit-for-tat strategy—can escalate, and often have escalated, into clan on clan warfare. Moreover, the *xeer* by itself is not well adapted to foster the joint development and shared use of resources among clans on an ongoing basis.[6] Traditional clan institutions that are internally democratic and adapted well to ensure the survival of a nomadic herdsman are often ill suited to cope with the needs of recurrent contact and lasting cooperation.

Somalia: A Failed Experiment with Statehood

The Republic of Somalia was formed in 1960 by joining, under the auspices of the United Nations, decolonized British and Italian Somalia.[7] A western democratic model of a state, centered in Mogadishu, was conceived, complete with a national assembly, a prime minister, and an elite bureaucracy.

Given the tradition of clan-based loyalties however, political associations immediately developed along clan lines; majority coalitions in parliament were realized by provoking disputes with other clan groups as a way of forming unity among one's own subclans. Following nine years of fratricidal clan politics, the army under General Siad Barre seized power in October 1969. Siad Barre proceeded to develop a highly centralized state along totalitarian lines. Clans and clan behavior were officially banned as unprogressive under the new "Scientific Socialism." An all-pervasive state machinery, inspired by that of North Korea, ruled directly through officials personally appointed by Siad Barre.

Barre himself presided over a revolutionary council composed of members from his, his mother's and his son-in-law's clans. He used tactics of divide and rule to stay in power, arming one clan group against the other. Thus, while on one hand destroying the constructive aspects of social capital that maintained relations among Somalis, Barre's policies exploited the weaknesses of clan structures for his personal advantage. Claiming to forge pan-Somali unity, he invaded the Ethiopian Ogaden in 1975. Although initially successful, the tide of the war turned and the retreating Somali army was followed by three-quarters of a million Ogadeni Somali refugees.

Even as the Ogaden war was seriously destabilizing the Somali state, the Soviet Union, eyeing a greater prize in Ethiopia, abandoned Somalia as its client state. Barre desperately turned to the West and, claiming that he was now fighting communism, sought weapons, foreign aid, and humanitarian assistance.

Despite massive quantities of aid, first from the Soviet Union and next from the United States, no effective development was measured; indeed, even though Somalis received per capita more aid than any other country, Somalia gained the reputation as a graveyard for aid (Ayittey 1997).

The Somali state finally collapsed in 1991. The Ogaden war, the practice of arming clans to fight other clans, and a civil rebellion by the nomadic clan groups in the north, upset in part at not having received their share of aid dollars from Mogadishu, all led to the fragmentation of the state. The humanitarian disaster that accompanied this prompted a military intervention by UNOSOM. Once again, attempts by the United Nations to reestablish a state along Western models belied a basic ignorance of local systems of collective action and ended in failure.

The effects of inter-clan conflict, exacerbated, first, by the requirements of majoritarianism and, next, by the divide-and-rule tactics of the Barre dictatorship, damaged traditions of cooperation *among* Somali clans, undermining traditional forums of accommodation *among* clan units. Moreover, efforts by Barre to outlaw clans and stamp out clan behavior debilitated the ability of traditional leaders to secure order *within* particular clan units.

Crafting New Institutions

Following the collapse of the Republic of Somalia in 1991, some former officials of the Mogadishu regime fled to Hargeissa, the capital of the erstwhile British Protectorate of Somaliland, and proclaimed the Republic of Somaliland. They drew up a constitutional charter that provided for, among other measures, a national currency, a flag, and the installation of a president and a council of ministers—selected from their own ranks.[8]

In the bitterness following the clan-on-clan conflict of the Somali civil war, clan-to-clan cooperation had effectively ceased. One result of this was that most of the communal lands and water sources, which had been maintained through the traditional system of covenanting, fell into disrepair. Still others were deliberately sabotaged over the course of the civil conflict. As viable common-pool resources became scarcer, additional conflicts arose over their shared use. The self-declared Somaliland government was not able to assert any order over this deteriorating situation.

In these bleak circumstances, several of the clan elders in Sanaag province realized that their traditional authority, though tattered, was the sole remaining constituting institution. Taking on the role of civic entrepreneurs, they convened a peace conference that drew on traditional conflict resolution practices to provide for restitution and reconciliation. For this peace to persist, many of the communal grazing lands and water resources that had been destroyed in war had to be rebuilt. The elders realized that the well-being of their own clans depended on the joint development and management of common pool resources with other clans. With memories of the conflict fresh on their minds, they were however, keenly aware of the challenge implied in this task.

The elders of Sanaag saw a practical way forward in the principles of institutional design introduced to them by Action Aid, a non-governmental organization. Drawing on criteria identified by Elinor Ostrom for successfully governing the commons, the elders began to recognize in their own traditions many of the same or similar principles of productive association.[9] In particular, the idea of compacting through the *xeer* was drawn on and extended to facilitate cooperation. New rules on sharing effort, monitoring use, and sanctioning non-compliance (among others) were agreed to—based on indigenous democratic norms of extensive debate and consensus agreement—prior to the release of building materials and other resources by donors.[10] As more communal resources were built, much of the conflict related to competition for scare water and grazing land also abated.[11]

These institution-building exercises gradually provided the clan elders and other members with much needed encouragement, experience, and confidence in their ability to craft the rules needed to govern the production and provision of public goods. Their experience with institutional analysis also equipped them with the tools to forecast potential problems of collective action and to articulate, in their terms of their own language, the rules needed to foster cooperation in rebuilding their destroyed infrastructure.

Building on their accomplishments, the clan elders came to recognize that many of the same principles of governance that apply to the construction and maintenance of a water reservoir or other physical asset could be applied to develop a broader set of more abstract institutions of government. Drawing on indigenous democratic norms of consensus-based decision making, they founded a Sanaag-wide Community Based Organization (CBO), which became the de facto point of orientation for multiple local initiatives in collective action (ranging from the provision of veterinary care to wireless telecom). The Sanaag CBO has since become the recognized government of Sanaag.

The relative success of clans in Sanaag in reconstruction and development has not gone unnoticed.[12] Elders, whose clans range in the neighboring province of Toghder, among others, have actively sought to learn from Sanaag's experience in order to foster their own "bottom-up" regional governance structures. In turn, these local governments have explored ways to cooperate with each other on issues of mutual concern.

Concurrently, government officials in the capital Hargeissa, finding that they had to deal with these regional governance structures, came to terms with the implied checks on their own declared authority.[13] This led to a call from the national and regional levels for a new national constitution that better reflected the new institutional arrangements. This constitution was approved in 2001 following national debate and a referendum. Somaliland has since held local and national elections and has seen a peaceful and constitutional transfer of its presidency.[14]

What appears to be emerging is an imperfect though functioning system of polycentric governance, rooted in the democratic norms of traditional clan governance and constrained through checks and balances that span across the political system. There is now a constitutional charter that reflects how the society is constituted.

These positive developments notwithstanding, there remain numerous potential developments that could prove destabilizing to Somaliland's constitutional accomplishments, including the discovery of oil and other natural minerals, the uncertain situation in the remainder of Somalia, and intervention by the outside world given the new geopolitics of terrorism in this strategically important area.

Constitution Design versus Constitutional Models

The idea of building up from and improving upon indigenous institutional resources for developing systems of collective action stands in contrast to the way in which constitutions have been drafted in the twentieth century when states, particularly those newly liberated from direct colonialism, overwhelmingly copied their imperial prototype in drawing up their political charters.[15] These constitutional models of Western democracies were seen to be worthy of emulation as they were associated with the progress and modernity of those societies.[16]

However, what was copied in these efforts in nation-building was the *form* in which problem-solving and collective decision-making were organized in the West, rather than the *principles* upon which they were derived from.[17] "Nation building" has usually meant setting up piece by piece the executive, legislative, and judicial branches of government, holding elections, and creating schools of public administration to train bureaucrats.

These would-be governance structures required individuals, who had ordered their relationships with others in their community in terms of long evolved and locally focused understandings, to reorient their political discourse in terms of foreign cultural expressions of democracy. They were to abandon centuries of tradition and experience in collective problem-solving and conflict resolution and were to now refer their problems to delegated policy experts, legislators, and bureaucrats within structures of governance that were not necessarily rooted in their own cultural dynamics.

A common result was that these government structures did not become facilities for problem-solving. Rather, as the modern history of Somalia and that of many other postcolonial states illustrates, these governments failed not only as institutions but also as organizations that produce and deliver basic services.

Crafting Good Governance

Good governance can take institutional root when it grows out of the problem-solving traditions of a society's indigenous institutions.[18] This bottom-up approach to developing a constitutional system contrasts with the top-down approach taken up by the elite of many of the states that emerged from colonial rule, where the formal constitutions of these states were often replicas of the constitutions of the former colonial power. As the example of Somalia tragically shows, the potential for indigenous institutions to evolve in a positive way to respond to contemporary problems was not nurtured in these cases. Instead, the inherent weaknesses of many of these indigenous institutions were often exploited as instruments of political control.[19]

For constitutions to be more than words on parchment, they must resonate understandings that are attuned to particular problem-solving communities. The hopeful experience of Somaliland points out that the passage to modernity for Africans and others lies not so much on fortifying the capacity of an abstraction called the state to function as an instrument for development but on rebuilding indigenous institutional potentials within a polycentric system of governance so that citizens, so constituted, may better craft and modify their problem-solving capabilities to adapt to new challenges and opportunities for self-realization and adaptive well-being.

CHAPTER 11

Toward a Democratic Civilization
for the Twenty-First Century

It has been frequently remarked that it seems to have been reserved to the people of this country, by their conduct and example, to decide the important question, whether societies of men are really capable or not of establishing good government from reflection and choice, or whether they are forever destined to depend for their political constitutions on accident and force.

Alexander Hamilton, *Federalist Papers*

The first duty which is at this time imposed upon those who direct our affairs is to educate the democracy; to warm its faith, if that be possible; to purify its morals; to direct its energies; to substitute a knowledge of business for its inexperience, and an acquaintance with its true interests for its blind propensities; to adapt its government to time and place, and to modify it in compliance with the occurrences and the actors of the age. A new science of politics is indispensable to a new world.

Alexis de Tocqueville, *Democracy in America*

Democracy is increasingly seen as the reality characterizing human civilization. In forging a new democratic world for the twenty-first century, a new science of politics is necessary—one that draws on human capacities to craft the rules of self-governance through reflection and choice. Indeed, human beings possess the potential to improve their well-being by devising rules governing their association with each other. Drawing upon mutual understandings, these rules shape behavior in situations where individuals can jointly realize opportunities to improve their well-being.

Rules, socially considered, are called institutions. When the existing institutions are missing or weak, or when the opportunity to generate and try out new solutions to shared problems is inadequate, the potential for humans to improve their well-being through collective action diminishes. A key challenge in constituting development, thus, concerns building the context necessary to encourage individuals to craft and try out new and locally relevant rules governing collective action.

A further challenge lies in reconciling each of these multiple (and potentially contradictory and overlapping) localized problem-solving initiatives within a broader political economy. This book has considered how locally focused institutions of governance—related within a polycentric constitutional system— can incorporate indigenous knowledge and shared understandings in crafting robust solutions to problems of collective action.

As we have seen, polycentricity describes a process of self-coordination among individuals at and among multiple centers, guided by locally relevant, broadly recognized, and non-arbitrary rules (Polanyi 1951). The polycentric approach to constitutional analysis, thus, recognizes that development is always a *local* phenomenon. Development can occur when individuals, realizing their potential through association with others, develop time-and-place specific rules to solve shared problems.[1]

In our quest to adapt, we strive to exploit and to reorganize the structures of both real and institutional resources in our environment in an attempt to improve, as we may imagine, our future adaptive prospects. This striving to adapt is a fundamental driving force of human behavior. Thomas Hobbes referred to this striving in his essay *Of Man*, observing, "the POWER *of a man*, to state it universally, is his present means, to obtain some future apparent good." In *Leviathan*, he observed as "a general inclination of all mankind, a perpetual and restless desire for power after power, that ceaseth only in death."

The capacity for humans to craft institutions draws on this broader notion of *power* as the potential for adaptive action by individuals to improve their future well-being by capitalizing on their association *with* others. Thinking about development from this perspective leads us to consider how public entrepreneurship can be motivated to build and strengthen local institutional resources.[2]

From State Governance to Constitutional Governance

In contrast to an understanding of development as a realization of adaptive potential by individuals through crafting rules for collective action, interpretations in the economics and public policy literature often see development in terms of a progression by a society from an earlier stage of maturation to a later stage of maturation. The expression "development," here, evokes a transformation from one set of circumstances—typically, those associated with poverty, malnutrition, and illiteracy—to another possessing the trappings of a rich society. Macroeconomic and aggregate social indicators are key tools, in this context, for tracking a country's transformation from "developing" to "developed" status.[3]

This aggregative approach to development vests the agents of a state with the prerogative of formulating and administering public policies intended to rapidly transform the economic and social characteristics of a country.[4] In systems of state-based governance, constitutions are recognized more as charters— parchments that set out the basic organization of a state's government and legitimize coercive action by a state's agents—than as frameworks for citizen engagement in problem-solving.[5]

Such systems of state-based governance, however, have been prone to failure, as the major constitutional experiments of the twentieth century confirm. Attempts at state-directed economic development and social change—based on Marx's vision of a new world—led to economic stagnation and widespread human misery in the Soviet Union, China, and other parts of the so-called Second World.[6] The reasons for the failure of the socialist state, as Friedrich Hayek (1945) explained, are systemic: centralized economic planning by a state is unfeasible since data gathered by the state cannot capture "time and place" knowledge possessed by individuals of their own exigencies. Furthermore, Hayek warned that a centralization of authority in the absence of effective constraints exposed state-governed societies to the perils of totalitarian dictatorship.[7]

A second set of constitutional experiments in state-led development involved societies that emerged newly independent of colonial rule in the middle part of the twentieth century. In forging new states, national leaders such as Nehru and Nyerere affirmed the prevailing ideological fashions of democratic socialism in presuming that a state, in the interest of its subjects, could diagnose problems and administer scientifically grounded policies to promote economic growth and social transformation (Nayar 1997).[8]

The field of development economics has since evolved to deal primarily with the challenges faced by these "Third World" states in fostering economic growth and social change.[9] A key element in this development landscape is international development assistance.[10] Yet, with more than fifty years of experience in this development enterprise, it is now increasingly recognized that the widespread failure of both policy remedies and financial assistance to promote transformative development in these societies is closely tied to the failure of the state.[11] This realization underpins major initiatives by leading donor agencies such as the World Bank to promote "Good Governance." Good Governance programs expect to revive the state by providing resources and training to improve its capacity for policymaking and public administration.[12] However, Good Governance itself is not likely to be sustainable given that the failure of development is rooted more fundamentally in the idea of the state itself.[13]

Vincent Ostrom (1973) has argued that the notion or contrivance of the state can lead to an "intellectual crisis in public administration" in that it stifles modes of creative inquiry and participation among citizens in solving problems of collective action. It follows that a study of development, when bounded within the concept of the state, limits intellectual efforts in seeking locally relevant ways by which individuals can improve their mutual well-being through exercise of their creative potentials.

Constitutional governance, in contrast to state governance, is consonant with citizens addressing their common needs through the freedom to integrate their actions with those of others within crafted rules and innovated institutional arrangements. Opportunities for citizens to realize their adaptive well-being is further enhanced, we have argued, when market and nonmarket institutions are relevant to local exigencies and draw on local knowledge and social understandings. Further, a stable political order can be organized along many of the same competitive principles associated with markets—to create the requisite checks and balances—while markets require an appropriate institutional infrastructure to be effective.[14] When processes of political and economic exchange are appropriately constrained within a polycentric constitutional system, citizens can be better equipped to address their mutual adaptive needs.

Achieving a Self-Governing Civilization

To realize a democratic civilization in this new century, we have to constitute self-governing societies where individuals as citizens are capable of participating effectively in the public realm. Self-governance is fundamental to development.

Alexander Hamilton's presumption in the *Federalist* was that societies of men and women can choose good government through reflection and choice, rather than depend on accident and force to produce their constitutions. He held that federalism (which describes a polycentric framework for self-governing societies) is first and foremost a political theory of citizenship.

Alexis de Tocqueville in *Democracy in America* argued, further, that a new age of democracy would only succeed to the degree that it developed a new political science—one based on principles of association, rather than one founded on the notion of a state.[15]

To achieve a vibrant self-governing civilization, we must replace the framework of state governance and public administration with a new understanding of constitutional governance and public entrepreneurship. This book is a modest attempt to further this understanding.

Notes

Chapter 1   Constituting Development

1. Margaret Levi (2002: 40) defines the state as "a complex apparatus of centralized and institutionalized power that concentrates violence, establishes property rights, and regulates society within a given territory while being formally recognized as a state by international forums."

2. Contemporary institutional analysts distinguish between incentive problems that arise from distortions in motivation (such as free riding and rent seeking) and asymmetries in information (such as the moral hazard problem and principal–agent problems). For a review, see chapter 3 and Gibson et al. 2005.

3. The free rider problem has long been recognized in the social sciences. See for example, David Hume 1975: Part II, Book 2.

4. Hardin (1968) provides the classic statement of the problem. For a review of our current knowledge about the importance of institutions in solving the tragedy of the commons, see National Research Council (2002).

5. Elinor Ostrom (2005) observes that "a major problem in understanding institutions relates to the diversity of situations of contemporary life."

6. I.M.D. Little (1982) argues that the experience of the Second World War in the United Kingdom shaped early debates on planning, with the state playing an instrumental role in setting clear goals and rapid implementation.

7. The French demographer Alfred Sauvy coined the expression "tiers monde" in French in 1952 by analogy with the "third estate." The third estate refers to the commoners of France before and during the French Revolution, in comparison to the priests and nobles, who comprised the first and second estates respectively. Thus, implicit in the term "Third World" is the idea that third world is exploited and that a change in its destiny is bound to be a revolutionary one. See Gerald Chaliand, "Third World" *Third World Traveler*, accessed on September 2004 at http://www.thirdworld traveler.com/General/ThirdWorld_def.html

8. Rosenstein-Rodan (1943) for example argued for a "big push." In his general critique of the state, Bartleson (2001: 182) notes that "the concept of the state came

to constitute a strategic resource and the very foundation of a modern science of politics by furnishing the quest for disciplinarity with identity, autonomy and authority."

9. See Ernest Stern (1944) for a description of the agreements that set up the World Bank and the International Monetary Fund.

10. Chapter 10 provides additional analysis of institutional failure and reconstruction in Somaliland.

11. While it is certainly true that these indigenous institutions, as given, may not provide well-adapted solutions to contemporary problems of collective action, they do provide the essential foundation for crafting new and viable institutions for social cooperation (Shivakumar 2003).

12. To Tocqueville, these mores contributed more to the maintenance of a democratic republic than the prevailing laws or other unique circumstances of the New World.

13. James Buchanan (1986: 271) notes that "any discussion of institutional change must embody the recognition *that we start from here*, and that *here* defines both time and place."

Chapter 2   Postwar Interpretations of Development

1. There is no attempt to provide a complete history of postwar development theory here. For further background, consult Colin Leys (1995), and Arturo Escobar (1996).

2. See for example, Wassily Leontief (1986).

3. Keynes' policies were first widely implemented in Britain to help finance the war effort. After World War II, they were quickly implemented in most of the western world, soon becoming the economic orthodoxy. Lawrence R. Klein (1980) represents the views of the growing consensus among postwar economists and government policy advocates.

4. For an excellent biography of Lord Keynes, see, Robert Skidelsky (2001).

5. In the case of India, Prime Minister Nehru embraced the idea of the state-led development as the key agent for national unity and nationalistic expression (Bose and Jalal 1997). A similar model was embraced by other new states such as Tanzania. Nayar (1972) further considers the role of the state in the Indian development context in the *Modernization Imperative*.

6. The Harrod-Domar model of growth provided a framework for economic planning that was promoted by P.C. Mahalanobis, the primary economic advisor to Prime Minister Nehru. The Mahalanobis model, which helped frame India's Second Five Year Plan (1956–1961), emphasized industrialization through self-reliance, and the dominant role of the public sector in basic and heavy industries. The Raj-Sen model subsequently strengthened Mahalanobis' model of planning, providing a theoretical underpinning to his contention that it is better to allocate scarce foreign exchange for importing machinery and technology to build up domestic capital capacity than to import the products of such capital equipment (Bose 1996). This focus on development planning led to a focus on means enhancement that lost sight of the

intended goal of a better life for Indians. This ideology of development marginalized the alternative Gandhian conception of a state of union forged from below that reflected and presided over the balance and harmony of free regional peoples and religious communities (Bose and Jalal 1997).

7. The target of halving the proportion of the world's poor by the year 2015 has been set by Kofi Annan, the UN Secretary General, at the UN Millennium Summit in April 2000 (*The New York Times* April 3, 2000. "In Report, Anan Sketches Future path of U.N.").

8. By equating development with output growth, early development theorists, prompted by Ragnar Nurske (1953), identified capital formation as the crucial component to accelerate development.

9. The state here implicitly refers to an internationally recognized legal entity with territorial sovereignty. For most developing countries, the constitution of this state refers to a document that sets out the form of government. These documents often borrow from western models, rather than reflect indigenous political understandings.

10. The reliance on the state as the instrument for change begs the question. After all, individuals in diverse ways have sought to improve their own lives in association with others before there were states and do so today even when there is no official state or when the state does not reach them.

11. This invites peculiar comparisons among states with different systems and characteristics, such as that between Singapore and Brazil.

12. "The ideological context in which Great Britain and France turned to development— the need to find a progressive basis for continued colonial rule in an era when major powers had made 'self-determination' a slogan of international politics—coincided with the heightened needs both had for their empires" (Cooper and Packard 1997).

13. Lord Keynes is considered by many to be the architect of the Bretton Woods system, with gave rise to the World Bank and the IMF. The impact of these organizations on development is a key part of the Keynesian legacy (Bordo and Eichengreen 1993).

14. USAID's presentation of its role in aid to India can be accessed at http://www.usaid. gov/in/specialfeatures/five_decades.htm.

15. Although the end of the Second World War represented the end of direct imperialism and, with the liberation of colonial peoples, the dawn of a new era in civilization, it can be argued that aid has sponsored a form of "crypto-imperialism" fostering degenerative tendencies in patterns of development (V. Ostrom 1988).

16. Paul Mosely (1987) has noted that "there appears to be no statistically significant correlation in any post-war period, either positive or negative, between inflows of development aid and the growth rate of GNP in developing countries when other causal influences on growth are taken into account."

17. Other issues related to ineffective and unsustainable aid include the scalability problem, where projects, successful in one context, fail in other, and the fungibility problem, where aid finance releases recipient country budgets for more marginal uses.

18. The semiconductor revolution, and in particular new telecommunications technologies, have created new international linkages among actors in developed and developing nations, with new implications for development. The current debate over offshore outsourcing (or off-shoring) is one manifestation of this rapid change. Lal (2000) provides an analysis of the institutional framework within which this globalization process is unfolding. See also recent studies by the Social Science Research Council on development and political economy, particularly with respect to globalization and local institutions, accessed at http://www.ssrc.org/programs/globallocal/

19. The OECD finds that foreign direct investment (FDI) in developing countries has risen sharply in recent years, becoming the most important source of external financing for some of them. See also http://www.bsdglobal.com/ngo/roles.asp on the rise of non-governmental organizations as a factor in development.

Chapter 3   The Aid Effectiveness Puzzle

1. This chapter is based on research by the author who, along with Krister Andersson, Clark Gibson, and Elinor Ostrom, conducted a study of aid, incentives, and sustainability for Sida, the Swedish bilateral aid agency, found in Ostrom et al. (2002). The authors subsequently expanded this analysis in Gibson et al. (2005).

2. Hansen and Tarp (2000) argue, for instance, that most of the macro studies over the last thirty years do in fact support the idea that aid helps national-level growth (see also Hansen and Tarp 2001). Other scholars still question the findings of these efforts, claiming that the two-gap theory upon which many statistical studies are based remains fundamentally flawed (Easterly 1999, 2003). While aid can certainly boast notable achievements (Levy 1987; Van de Walle and Johnston 1996), most scholars and practitioners would at least agree that it is too often ineffective (Elgström 1992; White 1992, 1998, 1999; Edgren 1995).

3. Good Governance has emerged as another key strategy to improve aid effectiveness. For a discussion, see chapter 5.

4. The leaders of recipient countries are also using the term in their efforts to examine critically their postindependence experience. The President of South Africa, Thabo Mbeki, and other African leaders have developed the Millennium African Renaissance Programme in which they call for all African leaders to "take ownership and responsibility for the sustainable economic development of the continent" (reported in *The Economist*, February 24, 2001, p. 17).

5. Institutions, in this way, are distinct from organizations. Organizations are, more simply, "groups of individuals bound by some common purpose to achieve objectives" (North 1990: 5). Simple organizations are those that can be analyzed as a separate action situation, where an action situation is a structured interaction where individuals must make decisions about actions that affect them and others. Complex organizations, in turn, are characterized by simultaneous and sequentially linked action situations. Organizations can take on institutional characteristics when the

rules of the organization increase the predictability of human interactions and thus make possible some activities that would not otherwise occur.

6. Since its formation in 1973, scholars affiliated with the Workshop in Political Theory and Policy Analysis at Indiana University have developed a useful theoretical tool called the IAD framework (Kiser and Ostrom 1982; Oakerson 1992; E. Ostrom et al. 1994; E. Ostrom 2005). The IAD framework has been employed in a large number of empirical studies, including those that measured the impact of metropolitan-area governance structures on urban service delivery, gauged how institutional incentives affect infrastructure sustainability in developing countries, examined how diverse forms of organization affect irrigation system performance, and explained how ecological conditions combined with institutional structure affect land use change dynamics (particularly changes in forest cover, extent, and composition) (see E. Ostrom et al. 1993; McGinnis 1999a and 1999b, 2000; Gibson et al. 2000). The IAD framework highlights how physical and material conditions, rules-in-use, and the attributes of community jointly shape policy outcomes.

7. When scholars analyze public goods problems formally, they generally assume that all participants have common knowledge about the costs of action and the distribution of benefits, that decisions about contributions are made independently (and frequently simultaneously), and that no external authority enforces potential agreements among actors. Public good situations formalized as a finitely repeated game with complete information generates actors that have a dominant strategy not to provide the good. Under the specified conditions, thus, the predicted outcome is that no one contributes and the public good is not produced (Roberts 1979). This outcome repeats in all finite repetitions. If uncertainty exists about the number of repetitions, the formal analysis generates a very large number of potential outcomes including zero contributions as well as full contributions. But the lesson to be learnt from these formal analyses is that unless the participants themselves are able to find ways of reaching enforceable agreements, or external authorities enforce effective rules, we should expect an inefficient provision of most public goods.

8. One of the most solid and empirically supported findings from the collective action literature is that without the development of adequate rules governing who will provide the good (and how), public goods will be undersupplied. Of course, such rules are themselves public goods, and can as such be under-provided.

9. In fact, education is an example of a public service that requires the active participation of both engaged parents and the students themselves in order to produce a good quality result. A donor has to be careful not to crowd out such necessary local engagement by providing too much support and thereby creating incentives to be passive observers among local people.

10. For an additional reference, see Ngaido and Kirk (2001) who provide an excellent review of the failed efforts of many African countries to solve rangeland problems through centralized interventions as well as the recent paradigm change to radical decentralization, which they argue will also be an inadequate institutional structure for a phenomenon that is complex and many layered.

11. Mancur Olson, on the other hand, theorized that groups with some advantaged members ("privileged groups") may in fact have an easier path to solving their collective-action problems. The better off individuals may contribute more than their fair share to solve the dilemma. But the solution reached may not benefit all equally or even in proportion to contribution. Empirical evidence for this contention is mixed. Part of the problem with applying this theory to the real world is the operationalization of privileged group. All communities have relatively richer and poorer members, but which should be considered privileged? How much should the difference in assets be to earn the attribute of privileged? These are challenging problems in operationalizing these concepts.

12. Hayek (1952), in his essay "Scientism and the Study of Society," refers to "Scientism" as the uncritical application of the methods, or of the supposed methods, of the natural sciences to problems for which they are not apt.

13. The "career concerns" models of Holmstrom (1982a and 1982b) and the multi-task model of Holmstrom and Milgrom (1991) examine what happens when agents are motivated more by the hope of demonstrating their abilities than by immediate monetary rewards. As Seabright (2002) argues, the strategic selection of which tasks to do and how to do them "is particularly applicable to the case of aid agencies who staff tend to be salaried rather than paid in a manner directly linked to ostensible performance." Convincing superiors that the work is outstanding leads to an input bias—that is more easily monitored—as contrasted to focusing on outcomes such as sustainability—which is far more difficult to monitor.

14. See chapter 10 for a case study of Somalia.

15. Hernando de Soto also clocked the amount of time that it takes a typical entrepreneur in Lima to get through all of the legal steps required to set up a sewing machine garment factory in Lima. "We discovered that to become legal took more than 300 days, working six hours a day. The cost: thirty-two times the monthly minimum wage" (2000: 189).

Chapter 4   The State as a Concept in Development

1. The idea of sovereignty is also associated with Jean Bodin, a sixteenth century French political absolutist philosopher, who asserted that a position of sovereignty exists in every state, and that the sovereign was limited only by his obedience to the law of God.

2. James M. Buchanan (1975: 68) views the leap from Hobbesian anarchy through negotiated agreement among individuals to limit predation and to cooperate in the production and provision of public goods. As such, he distinguishes between the protective and the productive roles of the state. The former role views the state emerging as "the enforcing agency or institution, conceptually external to the contracting parties and charged with the single responsibility of enforcing agreed-on rights and claims along with contracts which involve voluntarily negotiated exchanges of such claims." In the latter role, the state is conceived as "that

agency through which individuals provide themselves with 'public goods' in post-constitutional contract." In the Public Choice perspective, a state is conceded the power to monopolize the use of coercive force in order to impose taxes, provide public goods, and deal with externalities and other interdependencies.

3. According to Hobbes (1960) those who exercise these prerogatives are as such above the laws they promote and therefore not accountable to them or to other persons in the commonwealth. Hobbes' sovereign thus stands distinct from his subjects. He is not answerable "but to God," and so is restrained only by his sense of duty and the trepidations of "natural punishments" that follow from the breach of God's Law.

4. See for example, Chenery (1971).

5. As Srinivasan (1985) notes in relation to the related neoclassical literature, "it was believed that a well-informed government motivated solely by social welfare can correct all these market failures through appropriate intervention and also provide public goods. Further, such government intervention will also promote distributional justice. And the literature is full of sophisticated analyses and recommendations in regard to optimal taxation of income and wealth, import tariffs, and taxes or subsidies on commodity inputs, outputs and primary factors. It is hard to say if governments of developing countries were influenced by this advice. But it is a fact that they intervened massively. More often than not, these interventions either proved to be ineffective or worse than the disease of market failure that they were meant to cure."

6. In referring to the state as centralized, we do not preclude the fact that a particular state, as constituted, may be "decentralized." We contrast decentralization not to centralization but rather to non-centralized or polycentric systems of collective action. The challenge then is to consider how such systems can gain coherence.

7. The analyst takes on the perspective of the *omniscient observer* who, as Adam Smith (2000: Part VI, Section II) noted, "seems to imagine that he can arrange the different members of a great society with as much ease as the hand arranges the different pieces upon a chess-board; he does not consider that the pieces upon the chess-board have no other principle of motion besides that the hand impresses upon them; but that in the great chess-board of human society, every single piece has a principle of motion of its own, altogether different from that which the legislature might choose to impress upon it. . . . Some general, and even systematical, idea of the perfection of policy and law, may no doubt be necessary for directing the views of the statesman. But to insist upon establishing, and upon establishing all at once, and in spite of all opposition, every thing which that idea may seem to require, must often be the highest form of arrogance. It is to erect his own judgment into the supreme standard of right and wrong. It is to fancy himself the only wise and worthy man in the commonwealth, and that his fellow-citizens should accommodate themselves to him, and not he to them."

8. Demsetz (1996) notes that the Pigouvian tradition in economics relies on an omniscient state to implement policy.

9. The next chapter challenges the competence of the State as an institutional basis for development.

10. The United Nations sets standards by which member nations are to develop their national statistics. Agreeing to these standards is a key condition for membership in the UN.

11. Platform for Action, Fourth World Conference on Women, Beijing 1995.

12. As Leontief (1982: 34) notes, "we need to provide the foundation of factual analysis and economic projection that would make democratic national planning possible. The political economy will continue to flail blindly unless we can uncover its interacting empirical realities and consider in what general directions it should move."

13. Although neoclassical economics, as based on its axiomatic foundations, appears to provide a scientific and objective basis for policy analysis, these methodological foundations leave it vulnerable to generate a variety of policy conclusions. Taking the New Chicago School variant of Rational Choice Theory for example, we find that it is based on a set of generating assumptions as well as on auxiliary assumptions, since the axiomatic guidelines are themselves insufficient to generate the price-quantity relationships that characterize models in economics. Specific auxiliary assumptions must be cited for particular applications. As such, it is as Herbert Simon (1987: 39)observes, "too easy within the neoclassical methodological framework to save theory from unpleasant evidence by modifying the auxiliary assumptions and providing a new framework within which the actor 'must have been operating.' " Hence, Simon concludes, Rational Choice, as usually applied, is an "exceedingly weak theory, as shown by the difficulty of finding a set of facts, actual or hypothetical, that cannot be reconciled with it."

14. Sir Alec Cairncorss (1985) noted in his AEA Richard T. Ely lecture that economic policymaking involves producers (economists) competing to supply a market and consumers (the policymakers) hoping to find their wants supplied. The analysis and advice given by economists is shaped by the rules of this market.

15. These bounds are usually taken as the given in the economic calculus of maximizing within constraints. In contrast, Constitutional Economics examines choice among constraints (Buchanan 1996).

16. Ludwig von Mises (1966: 39) in *Human Action* notes that complex phenomenon becomes intelligible only through theories developed from other sources—"Without theory, the general aprioristic science of Human Action, there is no comprehension of the reality of human action." According to Hayek (1952a), we need a theory before we can ascertain if things behave as we would predict it. Pattern prediction thus involves forming a provisional hypotheses, forming a question, and employing our intellect to solve the problem.

17. The term "high theory," if used punctiliously, refers to the development of a style of general theoretic economics developed around the period of the Second World War by Robinson, Chamberlin, Pareto, Keynes, and other economists. The term here is employed to signify more broadly a highly theoretical, formalized, and mathematical,

economic and social theory that significantly abstracts from the economizing and exchange relationships in various contexts that characterize the problem-solving activities of human beings in the real world.

18. In his Presidential address delivered before the London Economic Club, Hayek noted that "I have long felt that the concept of equilibrium itself and the methods which we employ in pure analysis have a clear meaning only when confined to the analysis of the action of a single person and that we are really passing into a different sphere and introducing a new element of altogether different character when we apply it to the explanation of the interaction of a number of different individuals."

19. In a nonstationary world with less than perfect information, such as the one that we inhabit, the equilibrium assumptions do not hold and price is not synonymous with value.

20. Some experts have called for the development of satellite national accounts, which would include calculations of the value of women's work using some variation of the Marxian labor theory of value—where they may, for example, impute value based on the time spent on a particular activity (See, e.g., Goldschmidt-Clermont 2000.).

21. In this regard, see James M. Buchanan's analysis of Fiscal Illusion (Buchanan 1999: chapter 10).

22. Tocqueville (2004) in the *Old Regime and Revolution* was very careful to show that the theories and political rationales promoting centralization in the Old Regime in France seemed to advance various interests, but ultimately produced a context at odds with most parts of that society. This context produced its own contradictions by divorcing theory from practice, resulting in dangerous collective delusions.

23. Mirowski argues that neoclassical economics is essentially a simulacrum of energy concepts current in the physics of the mid-nineteenth century. Mirowski traces the history of the use of the physics metaphor to chide the profession for not developing much beyond its metaphoric constraints, even as physics has moved on. He notes that the reliance of the physics metaphor was a conscious attempt to appropriate to the social sciences the legitimacy accorded to the natural sciences.

24. The relationship between democracy and development is often addressed in the context of the so-called development-democracy-growth hypothesis. Observations center on the level of development and associated prevalence of democratic institutions and on whether the rate of growth is affected by the prevalence of democratic institutions. Pourgerami and Nelson and Singh cite various empirical studies that make arguments on both sides, without resolution. These studies all fail to appreciate the meaning of democracy as it pertains to problem-solving and development (Pourgerami 1998; Nelson and Singh 1998).

25. Fareed Zachariah (2004) notes that democracy without constitutional liberalism is producing centralized regimes, leading to an erosion of liberty, ethnic competition, conflict, and war.

26. Woodrow Wilson (1981) in *Congressional Government, A Study in American Politics* noted that "the natural and inevitable tendency of every system of self-government

like our own and the British is to exalt the representative body, the people's parliament, to a position of absolute supremacy." Wilson's central thesis in *Congressional Government* is that "the predominant and controlling force, the centre and source of all motive and all regulative power, is Congress."

27. Indeed, Hayek drew on Tocqueville's phrase, "the road to servitude," in coining the title for his book, *The Road to Serfdom.*

28. Development theory in the postwar period did not link development with democracy, although the issue was raised by Lipset (1959). See also Diamond et al. 1999.

Chapter 5   The State as the Means to Development

1. Martin Doornbos (2003) traces the evolution of "Good Governance" from a responsible handling of development assistance to recent fashions regarding selectivity to prequalify for aid.

2. As noted in chapter 1, the context of the postwar period prompted state-led solutions to the problems of underdevelopment. The exigencies of time and the apparent coherence of administrative centralization provided the basis for a long-standing framework of development analysis.

3. For a brief history of Development Economics, see Browne 1997.

4. For a critique of the gap approach to development, see William Easterly 1999.

5. When Somalia was abandoned by the Soviet Union as a client state in favor of the bigger prize of Ethiopia, the Somali dictator, Siad Barre turned to the United States, casting Somalia as a bulwark against Ethiopian Marxism. During this period, Somalia received the highest amount of aid per capita (Ayittey 1994). There is little evidence of the positive effect of that aid today. Chapter 10 discusses a constitution for development in the Somali context.

6. For an analysis of the political economy of aid in the donor country, see Philip R. Jones 1995. The British colonial development was first realized by the Colonial Development Act of 1929. Subsequently, a Ministry of Overseas Development was set up in October 1964. This ministry consolidated the functions of the former Department of Technical Co-operation and the overseas aid policy functions of the Foreign, Commonwealth Relations and Colonial Offices, and of other government departments. See also, L.C.A. Knowles 1936.

7. It should be noted that development administration had emerged as a sub-discipline in the early 1960s, though with emphasis on the improvement of government organizations involved in development as planners and implementers of policy. See Farazmand 2001.

8. It should also be noted that western aid during the cold war did pose (effectively) political conditions—that of not doing business with the communist bloc or adopting communist models.

9. For a skeptic's perspective of globalization, see Joseph Stiglitz 2002.

10. For an econometric analysis of the role of FDI in recent Chinese economic growth, see Tian 1997. The author, unable to distinguish between FDI led growth and growth led

FDI, concludes that FDI inflow and growth are likely mutually reinforcing. In comparison to East Asia, African countries have not seen major increases in foreign direct investment since the collapse of the Soviet Union, except for certain sectors like oil.

11. See, for example, *The Economist*, "The Whiff of Rotting Tyranny," January 16, 2003, for a report on the unrest in Zimbabwe.

12. The change in outlook of the Bank and IMF however tends to be portrayed more as an intellectual realization of the merits of the emerging "neo-liberal ascendancy" and as a result of the lessons learned from the structural adjustment policies carried out in the 1980s. This observation is based on conversations with current and former Bank officials. See also Leftwich 1994.

13. As an example of this interest, the third annual meeting of the International Society for New Institutional Economy, held in Washington DC on September 1999, was hosted by the World Bank. See www.isnie.org/ISNIE99.htm.

14. Williams (1996) notes that efforts to improve governance of developing countries rely largely on transplanting disciplinary techniques—such as surveys, audits, and due process—found in the developed world.

15. Kuldeep Mathur (2001) notes that the Good Governance view draws on a romantic view of civil society "where the existence of institutions outside the state become a sufficient basis to assume that state power is curbed and greater democratization is taking place. Such a perception does not take into account the characteristics of a society where there are associations, those of caste or of a religion, that exist primarily to curb the human rights of individuals."

16. For a critique of decentralization as a remedy for state failure, see Elinor Ostrom 2000.

17. A review of the 1997 *World Development Report* reveals less resistance to administrative decentralization, which involves the transfer of the state's coercive powers from higher to lower levels of government, while retaining centralized control of budgets and policymaking.

Chapter 6   The Constitutional Foundations of Development

1. As elaborated in chapter 10, indigenous institutions, as they have evolved (and particularly as they have been affected by the last half-century of postcolonial rule) may not necessarily represent efficient bases for systems of political association. Even so, they do represent the customs by which individuals in those societies relate to each other. They constitute the institutional reality and must be dealt with as such.

2. Mbaku (1998) notes that "Perhaps more important was the fact that constitution making in the pre-independence period was dominated and controlled by (i) the colonial state; (ii) resident European entrepreneurs, including settlers—especially in colonies such as South Africa and Southern Rhodesia; and (iii) a few Europeanized indigenous urban elites. These three groups were not well informed on social, political, and economic conditions in the rural sections of the colonies. This top-down, non participatory approach to constitutionalism resulted in institutional

arrangements that have since contributed significantly to poverty and deprivation in the African countries."

3. As Sen (1999a: 131) notes, "The informational focus of poverty analysis in this work has involved a shift from low income to deprivation of basic capabilities. The central argument for this shift is fundamental rather than strategic." Sen's insights on the relevance of freedom echo those of Friedrich Hayek (1960) in The *Constitution of Liberty*, in setting out the value of freedom with respect to human creativity and self-realization.

4. This examination of the constitutional experience of the United States is not an endorsement of the US constitutional model. Indeed, US constitutional history has several rather dismal chapters, including that on slavery and the treatment of the native population. Our focus on Tocqueville is to draw on his method of comparative constitutional analysis.

5. In noting that he considers mores to be "one of the great general causes responsible for the maintenance of a democratic republic in the United States," Tocqueville (2000) elaborates that he means it "to apply not only to "morals" in the strict sense, which might be called the habits of the heart, but also to the different notions possessed by men, the various opinions current among them, and the sum of ideas that shape mental habits." In all, the concept of mores is developed to illuminate certain intellectual underpinnings in American society that help support its political institutions.

6. By contrast, Cameroon's Constitution, drafted according to the French model, was a product of political exigency, reflecting an eagerness to forgo deeper constitutional deliberations in order to accelerate the process of decolonization (Mbaku 1998).

7. The trajectories of some of states' institutions were to lead to the sort of problematic "state-monopoly" tendencies to which Tocqueville objected. Tocqueville's difficulty with some state constitutions in this regard was earlier voiced by Thomas Jefferson (on whose work Tocqueville directly and indirectly relied) and by Madison, forming, in part, the argument between "Federalists" and "Anti-federalists." Indeed, several framers of the US Constitution benefited from their knowledge of the states' experience and tried to create a better *constitutional system*, where the US Constitution and state constitutions complement each other. The issue is thus not one of whether—for any principled reason—national constitutions are better than state constitutions, or vice versa. The author is grateful to Barbara Allen for this clarification.

8. For a description of nineteenth Century US Machine Politics, see Slater 1974.

9. The Progressive Movement was a campaign for economic, political, and social reform in the United States, often dated as beginning in the 1890s and ending in 1917 with the entry of the United States in First World War. Among the political reforms of this period were new laws concerning voter recall, referenda, state primaries, and the direct election of US senators to help counter problems related to corrupt governance. (See Scopino 1997.) Key among the institutional reforms of the Progressive Movement was a constitutional amendment calling for the direct election of senators to the US Congress. Indeed, the earlier indirect election of senators to the US

Congress was a major institutional force contributing to Boss Rule and other negative developments in the states' political cultures.

10. "Among the laws that rule human societies there is one which seems to be more precise and clear than all others. If men are to remain civilized or to become so, the art of associating together must grow and improve in the same ratio in which the equality of conditions is increased." (See Tocqueville 2000: Book II, Chapter 5.)

11. "That is the source of our fellow-feeling for the misery of others, that is by changing places, in fancy with the sufferer, that we come either to conceive or to be affected by what he feels, may be demonstrated by many obvious observations, if it should not be thought sufficiently evident of itself" (Adam Smith, *Moral Sentiments* I.1).

12. Thomas Hobbes, in his essay *Of Man* notes:. "Weighing the actions of other men with his own, they seem too heavy, . . . put them into the other part of the balance, and his own into their place, that his own passions, and self-love, may add nothing to the weight; and then there is none of these laws of nature that will not appear unto him very reasonable."

13. Even as the capacity for sympathy is common to all, cultural perspectives, that emerge from problem-solving in varied contexts, are somewhat more diverse. Thus, while language is a universal feature of human civilization, language itself is variable. Yet, even as language has the capacity to amplify human potentials, we continue to rely primarily on our resources as human beings to understand the language and cultural achievements of others (V. Ostrom 1997).

14. As Barbara Allen (2005) has noted, Tocqueville made clear that it was the specific federal theologians of Reformed Protestants who took up covenanting and carried the religious mode of voluntarism into the particular secular forms of American federalism. The democratic revolution had changed catholicism, so that American catholics could accept some forms of protestant voluntarism. But Tocqueville did not view the institutions established by American catholics as covenantal. He called Virginians the "other branch" of the Anglo-American family, in part because of their creation of a slaveholding society, but also because he viewed Anglicanism as much less "federal" and much more hierarchical than New England Puritanism.

15. Daniel Elazar (1995) in *Covenant & Commonwealth* suggests that Muhammad employed a covenantal orientation in politics, but that his followers found such a connection of Biblical covenant and worldly association by consent and disputation easy to dispense with. Elazar asks if the religion constituted by such followers is still amenable to covenant, just as he asks if the Christianity contemplated in the notion of apostolic succession, papal infallibility, etc. of Catholicism still amenable to covenantal modes.

16. Elazar (1995) points out that the covenant is one of three great approaches to human organization and that most societies are mixtures of the major modes: covenant-reflection and choice/federal matrix, conquest-force/hierarchy and organic (kinship)-fate/center-periphery.

17. The utilitarian criterion for judging social actions and institutions associated with the names of Jeremy Bentham James Mill, and F.Y. Edgeworth was perhaps captured best by Sidgwick (1973) "By utilitarianism is here meant the ethical theory that the conduct which, under any given circumstances, is objectively right, is that which will produce the greatest amount of happiness of the whole; that is, taking into account all whose happiness is affected by the conduct."

Chapter 7   Adaptive Development and Institutional Problem-Solving

1. Rizzello and Turvani (2000) note that the importance of the connection between the evolution of the mind and the evolution of institutions highlights the need to investigate the cognitive mechanisms of individuals.
2. Popper (1972: 261) observed that "The difference between the ameba and Einstein is that the ameba dislikes to err. . . . while Einstein is intrigued by it: he consciously searches for his errors in the hope of learning by their discovery and elimination. The method of science is the critical method."
3. The bounded rationality model recognizes that the process of problem-solving in itself may give rise to new problems that require attention. The problem-solver has then the option either to switch to the new task or to concentrate on the initial problem. As such problem-solving was conceptualized, as per early understandings in Artificial Intelligence Theory, as a serial operation where the mental processor evokes only one method at a time (Simon 1962).
4. As his obituary in the journal *American Psychologist* points out, "although Hayek's works have clear relevance for both theoretical and applied issues in psychology, this has only rarely been acknowledged" (Mahoney and Weimer 1994). See also Weimer 1982.
5. Hayek, 1952a, p. 111.
6. David Hume in discussing the problem of induction in *Human Understanding*, differentiates "impressions" from "ideas" and points out that it is custom and not reason that ultimately is a guide to life.
7. "The first proponent of cortical memory networks on a major scale was neither a neuroscientist nor a computer scientist but . . . a Viennese economist: Friedrich von Hayek (1899–1992). A man of exceptionally broad knowledge and profound insight into the operation of complex systems, Hayek applied such insight with remarkable success to economics (Nobel Prize, 1974), sociology, political science, jurisprudence, evolutionary theory, psychology, and brain science (Hayek 1952a)" (Joaquin Fuster 1995: 87). Also see J.L. Elman 1993: pp. 71–99. Finally see W. Brian Arthur et al. 1997.
8. The features listed have been repeatedly invoked in the literature on institutional analysis. See e.g.: Ludwig Lachmann 1971; Geoffrey Brennan and James M. Buchanan 1985; Richard Langlois 1986 and Douglas North 1990.

9. Cooperation is usually analyzed in game theory by means of a non-zero-sum game called the "Prisoner's Dilemma." The two players in the game can choose between two moves, either "cooperate" or "defect". The idea is that each player gains when both cooperate, but if only one of them cooperates, the other one, who defects, will gain more. If both defect, both lose (or gain very little) but not as much as the "cheated" cooperator whose cooperation is not returned. See Robert Axelrod 1984.

10. Mengerian explanations typically account for the emergence of coordinative solutions.

11. The axioms of Rational Choice Theory, in this regard, provide constraining criteria to model decision-making.

12. This distinction is set out within the Institutional Analysis and Development (IAD) Framework for an introduction to the IAD, see Elinor Ostrom et al. 1994.

13. Imre Lakatoš' Methodology of Scientific Research Programmes (1970) envisages a hard core and a protective belt—that is a core set of propositions and associated assumptions and conditions that can absorb the impact of contradictory evidence.

14. For an analysis of the development of the theory of interest from earliest times, through the medieval usury doctrine, to the nineteenth century, see Eugen von Böhm Bawerk 1890.

15. Vanberg (1994) sets out this distinction in discussing group selection, particularly with respect to that which might be seen as implied in Hayek's later works. Vanberg's reinterpretation of Hayekian Cultural Evolution stresses the role of conditioning criteria and points out that this clarification is consistent with the tenor of Hayek's life-work.

Chapter 8 Institutions, Market Exchange, and Development

1. The importance of institutions for markets is highlighted in the World Bank's 2002 *World Development Report*.

2. The phrase, "government failure," is often understood to imply that government will necessarily do things in a less efficient way than the market. More appropriately, it reflects the idea that governmental organizations, no less than other social or commercial enterprises, are prone to failures of collective action. See also Krueger 1990.

3. See for example, Hodge 2002. For an analysis of the impact of the privatization of British Rail, see Pollitt and Smith 2001.

4. Relatedly, Gambetta (1993) analyzes the sicilian mafia as a cartel providing "protection," or guarantees that underwrite business and social transactions.

5. For a summary of the development of these and other core ideas of the new Austrian school from its beginnings in Vienna in the 1870s to the present, see Vaughn 1991.

6. Eight former independent domestic airlines; Deccan Airways, Airways-India, Bharat Airways, Himalayan Aviation, Kalinga Air Lines, Indian National Airways, Air India, Air Services of India, were merged to form the new domestic national carrier.

7. For a brief history of Indian Airlines, see http://airlines.afriqonline.com/airlines/426.htm and http://www.indian-airlines.nic.in/

8. Steering clear of these extremes, they held that, as Willgerodt and Peacock (1989) put it in their review of German Ordo-Liberalism, "the rule of law together with the legal and social framework must circumscribe both spontaneous processes and the activities of the state."

9. In the next chapter, we note that the characteristics of a social order are shaped by circumscribing political institutions. Developing a desirable state of affairs may require reconstituting these institutions.

10. "In its essentials, a market system is one in which, as far as possible, all goods that people might want are private property; property rights in these goods are well defined, freely divisible, and freely exchangeable. It is immediately obvious that this system has a built-in dynamic of wealth creation. If any group of two or more individuals become aware that they all can become better off by reallocating their property rights between themselves, then the members of this group have the power to bring the improvement about. The fact that this is true of *every* set of individuals in an economy generates an extremely dense network of potential trading relations and a vast degree of redundancy" (Sudgen 1998a).

11. As Müller-Armack (1989) notes, "apart form the social functions which are more or less inherent in a system of competition, it is also possible under this system to take care of other social needs."

12. A market order in the absence of conditioning criteria can take on aspects of a Hobbesian jungle. Here, each party would have to expend resources to fend off offensives by others. In such cases, the wealth creating potential of a market would be stunted since the costs of transacting in such a market would be prohibitive. Recognizing the mutual benefit to be gained through limiting such behavior, individuals can negotiate agreements, characterized by enforceable precommitments to limit defense and predation. From this, law can emerge with each person accepting the limits to his or her own freedom in some areas to liberate action in other spheres. Such an argument is consistent with that drawn by Buchanan (1975). The emergence of the *Law Merchant* provides one example of how such rule of market can emerge spontaneously. It is also possible to imagine that such rules can be the result of pragmatic choice and deliberated negotiation (Berman 1983 and Benson 1990).

13. Buchanan (1975: 95) distinguishes between the *protective state* and the *productive state*: "I have called that part of government which acts as the enforcing institution of society, the 'protective state' and that part of government that facilitates public goods exchanges the 'productive state.' "

14. Eucken (1952) specifies monetary stability, private ownership of the means of production, freedom of contract, responsibility for economic decisions, and stability in economic policy as preconditions for a well-functioning market economy.

15. Hutt (1940) coined the term *consumer sovereignty*. The notion also resonates in the Austrian literature. For example, Mises (1966: 269–273) notes that consumers determine, in their own changeable and unpredictable way, what has to be produced. Manufacturers and retailers would go out of business if they did not organize

their factors of production and provide better and cheaper goods to satisfy their customers.

16. The next chapter captures a parallel argument with respect to political decentralization in the absence of meaningful constitutional constraints.

17. For example, the delivery of public services can be structured in terms of market-like competitive arrangements. Solving problems of governance rest on adopting principles of polycentricity; as Ostrom and Ostrom (1977) conclude, "competitive pressures are the key factors in maintaining the viability of a democratic system of public administration."

Chapter 9 Crafting the Institutions for a Problem-Solving Society

1. "To say that the order is spontaneous is to say that in some sense the elements have *arranged themselves* into order. . . . For the elements to be able to arrange themselves, each must act on its own principles of behavior or laws of motion; the regularity among the set of elements must be capable of being explained by the individual actions of the elements. This requires that each element have its own motive power, or be acted on by its own set of forces" (Sudgen 1998b).

2. "Generally speaking, the mutual adjustments required for the establishment of a competitive economic order must be initiated by individual agents empowered to dispose of resources and products, subject to general rules; these mutual adjustments are bargains concluded through the market; the application of general rules to conflicts between bargainers constitutes the legal order of private law, which itself is a system of mutual adjustments. Economic liberty and an important range of juridical independence thus jointly form the institutional basis for the social performance of an economic task of a polycentric character" (Polanyi 1951: 186).

3. Within modern political science literature, the effectiveness of polycentric systems, and the organization of public economies as a complement to market economies, is most systematically and rigorously elaborated in the context of metropolitan governance. The Workshop in Political Theory and Policy Analysis, in conducting extensive empirical studies on policing in metropolitan areas, has clearly established the problem-solving superiority of polycentric as opposed to unitary systems of governance. A system of governance for metropolitan areas based on many competing, sometimes overlapping centers of decision-making, each reflecting locally relevant scale and scope, and emphasizing local participation in formulating charters for self-governance and the resolution of problems of collective action was found by the affected citizens to be more effective than the centralized production and provision of city services. A review and analysis of this considerable empirical undertaking is provided by Elinor Ostrom (1997) in her acceptance paper for the Seidman award. Other areas of extension for the principle of Polycentricity include market systems, judicial decision-making, constitutional rule, and the selection of political leadership.

4. In *Federalist 47*, Madison quotes Montesquieu's contention from *The Spirit of the Laws*: "When a legislative power is united with executive power in a single person or in a single body of the magistracy, there is no liberty."

5. The literature on decentralization is extensive. There is no attempt here to be comprehensive.

6. More often than not, decentralization has failed to spur the reality of development. Even its early champions have expressed their disappointments at the failure. See G.S. Cheema and D.A. Rondinelli, eds., *Decentralization and Development: Policy Implementation in Developing Countries*, Beverly Hills CA: Sage Publications, 1983.

7. In fact, little can be said empirically about the relationship between decentralization and growth. As the World Bank (2003) concludes, "From this point of view, the design of decentralization becomes the key factor in determining whether policies will lead to the efficiency linked to higher growth, exacerbate the deficits and instability connected to lower growth, or simply become mired in institutional constraints." See http://www.worldbank.org/publicsector/decentralization/impacts.htm.

8. Decentralization is often attempted in terms of the overt features of polycentric governance—but often without addressing the institutional constraints underpinning it. In cases where the institutional support exits, it may work; otherwise, it may fail. It is therefore possible to argue without resolution for and against decentralization, if its institutional foundations are not understood.

9. These inevitable puzzles pose fundamental challenges. In rising to these challenges we may be guided by a norm that poses that it is the individual who is the ultimate sovereign in appraising the outcomes of social choice. As social scientists, we too are engaged in problem-solving as constrained within disciplinary and sub-disciplinary rules. As such, we have observed that when social choices among and within rules are constrained by Normative Individualism, patterns of order are created which are congruent with advanced human development and economic progress. For a discussion of Normative Individualism in Constitutional context, see Vanberg 1986, and Buchanan 1988.

10. See in particular the discussion in chapter 4 of this volume.

11. As Olson (1971) noted, "Unless the number of individuals is quite small, or unless there is coercion or some other special device to make individuals act in their common interest, *rational, self-interested individuals will not act to achieve their common or group interests.*"

12. This section has been enriched through discussions with Stephan Kuhnert. See Kuhnert 2001.

13. Figure 2 in chapter 7 provides a schematic diagram of institutional problem-solving.

14. This includes markets as a forum of collective problem-solving. See chapter 8 for an elaboration of this point.

15. Traditional economic approaches view maximization as within given constraints. The constitutional viewpoint however incorporates an analysis of these constraints themselves. In the absence of this constitutional perspective, innovation in traditional treatments is introduced by exogenous means.

16. To be sure, public entrepreneurs are aware of how these rules, as may be played out, can affect their own fortunes, as we see next.

Chapter 10   Crafting New Institutions on Indigenous Foundations

1. Highlighting a key aspect of this neglect of institutional realities, Hernando de Soto (2000) argues that the indigenous property rights institutions of the poor in many developing countries is not officially recognized, hampering their developmental potential.
2. For a classic articulation of this view, see Friedman 1953.
3. As we argued in chapter 4, problem-solving in this tradition is consigned to the state. After all, if there is a universal rationality, then it follows that there should be a unitary forum for problem-solving and conflict resolution. Accordingly, the state is vested with monopoly prerogatives in collective problem-solving and conflict resolution. This approach is particularly prominent, if often implicitly so, in recommendations found within much of the Development Economics literature.
4. As Buchanan (1986: 271) notes, "any discussion of institutional change must embody the recognition *that we start from here*, and that *here* defines both time and place." For a restatement of the importance of the status quo as a starting point, see James Buchanan 2004.
5. The analysis based in part on extensive interviews and discussions with traditional leaders from Sanaag and Toghder and with parliamentarians and senior government officials of Somaliland in June 1998, July 1999, and March 2001.
6. Lacking this institutional infrastructure, development aid projects that seek to install infrastructure such as water reservoirs were prone to fail.
7. For a more detailed history, see Lyons and Samatar 1995.
8. For a more detailed account of institutional building in Somaliland, see Bradbury et al. 2003.
9. The design principles identified by Elinor Ostrom (1990) include delineating clear boundaries, establishing congruence of rules and local conditions, including participation by most of those affected, appointing monitors accountable to participants, developing sanctions for rules breakers that are graduated, providing readily available ways of resolving disputes, ensuring that rights are not challenged by authorities, and developing rule structures in nested arrangements.
10. The underlying collective-action problem was addressed before the donor provided assistance, greatly improving prospects for aid sustainability.
11. Indeed, terms such as "collective action" also entered their lexicon.
12. While there have been significant gains in developing elements of an effective system of polycentric governance and momentum in this regard remains positive, the extent of success in this regard is difficult to predict. As we would expect, this process, as any exercise in constitutional development, is complex. Interviews and personal conversations with diverse individuals in Somaliland reveals, as one would expect, a

range of interests in and theories about a future constitutional order. The fragile process of constitutional development is also susceptible to buffeting from outside, particularly with considerable new external interest—in this era of terrorism—in this geo-politically sensitive region.

13. The lack of international recognition has played an important role in the bottom-up constitutional development of Somaliland. Absent official development aid, which can come only with international recognition, the national government has not enjoyed an advantage in dealing with the regions, helping to create balance on its power.

14. Elections for district councils were held in December 2002, followed by presidential elections in April 2003.

15. In the case of Cameroon, Mbaku (1998) points out that adopting the French model was a product of political exigency and an eagerness to forgo deeper constitutional deliberations in order to accelerate the process of decolonization.

16. Ayittey (1994a) notes the particular fascination among the African elite of western ways of doing things: "These modernizing African clung to the notion that anything traditional was by definition primitive. And it was this elite that came to the fore-front of the independence movements and proceeded to impose European models on their new African states."

17. As McCloskey (1987) notes, the metaphor of "nation-building" suggests an effort in construction where the elements of governance can be assembled brick by brick.

18. Tocqueville (2000) pointed out that the United States system of governance grew out of local traditions in covenanting and initiative in problem-solving. Even so, these capabilities are being eroded through the introduction of unitary forms of collective problem-solving (V. Ostrom, 1997). In the case of the initial crafting of United Sates Constitution, stakeholder groups did not include the slave population. Other exceptions can be found among Western constitutions.

19. Ayittey (1987) notes the incongruity between the indigenous value systems and the policy environment that peasants find themselves confronting: "In relative terms, the traditional environment is of greater importance, because illiterate people tend to go more by custom and age-old practices than by national policies they may not understand."

Chapter 11   Toward a Democratic Civilization for the Twenty-First Century

1. According to Sen's (1999) "capability freedom" perspective, "the institutional arrangements for these opportunities are also influenced by the exercise of people's freedoms, through the liberty to participate in social choice and in making of public decisions that impel the progress of these opportunities." Sen's view that well-being is secured through freeing the individual to be involved in and making decisions regarding his or her own life raises the question of how are we to conceive of a compatible system of government. See chapter 6 of this book for an analysis of this point.

2. Hobbes believed that unconstrained competition for scarce resources would lead to conflict—a state of war of "every man against every man," where self-interest narrowly pursued leads to misery. For Hobbes, a sovereign, representing a unity of power *over* his subjects was needed to forestall this anarchy. The distinction between *power with* and *power over* is an important point of departure.

3. The World Development Indicators, published annually by the World Bank provides classifications and statistics on a broad range of measures that distinguish poor countries from rich ones. See http://econ.worldbank.org/wdr/. A composite index that goes beyond per capita income is described in *Human Development Report*, published by the United Nations Development Programme. See http://hdr.undp.org/

4. Though recognizing the role of institutions in "shaping the quality and effectiveness of growth," the 2002 *World Development Report* still relies on the idea of the state as an indispensable agent for development: "In many areas, government plays a central role in organizing dispersed interests: meeting national goals and balancing competing interests. Unlike social norms and values, government operates a rule-making process by which the rules can be changed more quickly, with vision and design, and still be forceful." (World Bank 2002: chapter 3).

5. James Madison in *Federalist 48* noted "that a mere demarcation on parchment is not a sufficient guard against those encroachments which lead to tyrannical concentration of all powers of government in the same hand." See also Wagner, 1993.

6. Soviet and Chinese experiments in collective farming resulted in very large famines. The tolls of the Soviet famines of 1921 and 1932–1933 are estimated at 5.1 million and 7 million deaths respectively (Conquest 1986). Estimates for the Chinese famine of 1958–1961 range from 30 to 40 million deaths (Becker 1996).

7. In his essay, "Why the Worst get on Top," Hayek (1994) points out that the unscrupulous and uninhibited are likely to be more successful in a society organized in terms of a centralized authority.

8. Scott (1998) provides a detailed account of the modernization program undertaken by Julius Nyerere in Tanzania that resulted in widespread bureaucratic bullying and state violence against its citizens, the destruction of viable communities and patterns of livelihood, and environmental devastation.

9. Keynes's legacy casts a long shadow on development economics. The policy agenda for state-directed development in many third world states is frequently expressed in the rhetoric of Keynesian analysis. Through his role in the inauguration of the Bretton Woods organizations, Keynes also left a lasting imprint on the architecture of international development assistance.

10. Aside from the humanitarian motive for development assistance, aid has long served other purposes. The framework of aid, in many cases, proved to be a basis for a donor country to continue dealings with a former colony or to establish new economic and political relationships in specific countries and regions of the world. As a means of securing strategic alliances with the rulers of poor countries, aid has also served other geopolitical exigencies in the cold war. In these respects, development aid reflects a form of "crypto-imperialism" (V. Ostrom 1988).

11. It is increasingly evident that development failure is not the only manifestation of the intellectual crisis of state governance. Modern tragedies of civil wars and famine provide stark evidence of societies that have failed to constitute themselves successfully within a state based framework of governance. Recent events in Afghanistan, Iraq, and Liberia underscore this reality. Further, as the 2001 terrorist attacks in the United States have exposed, the implications of state failure are no longer contained within the so-called Third World. A pressing global challenge today, therefore, is to rethink what constitutes development so as to reconstitute the problem-solving institutions of healthy and productive societies.

12. The interest in good governance was heralded by a 1989 World Bank publication, Sub-*Saharan Africa: From Crisis to Sustainable Growth*. For an analysis of state failure and its impact on growth in Sub-Saharan Africa, see Collier and Gunning, 1999.

13. See chapter 5 of this book for a critique of Good Governance as conceived by the World Bank and the United Nations Development Programme.

14. See chapter 9 of this book.

15. Likewise, Vincent Ostrom (1997) observes that "democracies are at risk when people conceive of their relationships as being grounded in command and control rather than on principles of self-responsibility in self-governing communities of relationship." See Ostrom, *The Meaning of Democracy and the Vulnerability of Democracies*, Ann Arbor: University of Michigan Press, 1997.

Bibliography

Akerlof, George A. 1970. "The Market for 'Lemons': Qualitative Uncertainty and the Market Mechanism." *Quarterly Journal of Economics* 84: 488–500.

Alchian, Armen A. 1950. "Uncertainty, Evolution, and Economic Theory." *Journal of Political Economy* 58(3): 211–221.

Alchian, Armen A. and Harold Demsetz. 1972. "Production, Information Costs, and Economic Organization." *American Economic Review* 62(5) (December): 777–795.

Alesina, Alberto and Roberto Perotti. 1994. "The Political Economy of Growth: A Critical Survey of the Recent Literature." *World Bank Economic Review* 8(3): 351–372.

Alexeev, Michael. 1999. "The Effect of Privatization on Wealth Distribution in Russia." *Economics of Transition* 7(2): 449–465.

Allen, Barbara. 2005. *Tocqueville Covenant and the Democratic Revolution: Harmonizing Earth with Heaven*. Lanham, MD: Lexington Press.

Arkadie, Brian Van. 1990. "The Role of Institutions in Development." In Stanley Fisher and Dennis de Tray, eds. *Proceedings of the World Bank Annual Conference on Development Economics, 1989*. Washington, DC: World Bank.

Arthur, W. Brian. 1994. "Inductive Reasoning and Bounded Rationality." *American Economic Review* 84: 406–411.

Arthur, W. Brian, Steven Durlauf, and David Lane. 1997. *The Economy as an Evolving Complex System II Series in the Sciences of Complexity*. Reading, MA: Addison-Wesley.

Axelrod, Robert. 1984. *The Evolution of Cooperation*. New York: Basic Books.

Ayittey, George B.N. 1987. Economic atrophy in Black Africa. *Cato Journal* 7(1): 195–222.

———. 1994a. "The Failure of Development Planning in Africa." In P.J. Boettke, ed. *The Collapse of Development Planning*. New York: NYU Press.

———. 1994b. "To Aid Africa, By-Pass the Autocrats." *The Wall Street Journal* (Europe), March 23, 1994, p. 9.

———. 1997. *Africa in Chaos*. New York: St. Martin's Press.

Bartelson, Jens. 2001. *Critique of the State*. Port Chester, NY: Cambridge University Press.

Bator, Francis. 1958. "The Anatomy of Market Failure." *Quarterly Journal of Economics* 72(2): 311–400.

Bauer, Peter T. 1971. *Dissent on Development; Studies and Debates in Development Economics*. Cambridge: Harvard University Press.

———. 1984. *Reality and Rhetoric*. London: Weiden Feld & Nicholson.

Becker, J. 1996. *Hungry Ghosts: Mao's Secret Famine*. New York: Henry Holt and Company.

Bell, Simon and Stephen Morse. 1999. *Sustainability Indicators: Measuring the Immeasurable*. London: Earthscan Publications.

Benson, Bruce. 1990. *The Enterprise of Law*. San Francisco: Pacific Research Foundation.

Berman, Harold. 1983. *Law and Revolution: The Formation of the Western Legal Tradition*. Cambridge, MA: Harvard University Press.

Bhagwati, Jagdish N. 1982. "Directly Unproductive, Profit-Seeking (DUP) Activities." *Journal of Political Economy* 90(5): 988–1002.

Blomstrom, Magnus and Mats Lundahl, eds. 1993. *Economic Crisis in Africa: Perspectives on Policy Responses*. New York: Routledge.

Böhm-Bawerk, Eugen von. 1890. *Capital and Interest: A Critical History of Economical Theory*, trans. William Smart. London: Macmillan.

Boone, Peter. 1994. "The Impact of Foreign Aid on Savings and Growth." Working Paper. London: London School of Economics.

———. 1996. "Politics and the Effectiveness of Foreign Aid." *European Economic Review* 40: 289–329.

Bordo, Michael D. and Barry Eichengreen. 1993. *A Retrospective on the Bretton Woods System: Lessons for International Monetary Reform*. Chicago: University of Chicago Press.

Bosc, Pierre-Marie and Ellen Hanak-Freud. 1995. *Agricultural Research and Innovation in Tropical Africa*. Paris: Centre de Coopération Internationale en Recherche Agronomique Pour le Développement.

Bose, Deb Kumar. 1996. "The Mahalanobis Model in Retrospect." In Manabendu Maiti Chattopadhyay and Mihir Pradip Rakshit, eds. *Planning and Economic Policy in India: Evaluation and Lessons for the Future*. New Delhi: Sage Publications.

Bose, Sugata and Ayesha Jalal. 1997. *Nationalism, Democracy, and Development*. Oxford: Oxford University Press.

Boychko, Maxim, Andrei Shleifer, and Robert Vishny. 1996. *Privatizing Russia*. Cambridge, MA: MIT Press.

Bradbury, Mark, Adan Yusuf Abokor, and Haroon Ahmed Yusuf, "Somaliland, choosing politics over violence," *Review of African Political Economy* 3(97): 455–478.

Brainerd, Elizabeth. 1998. "Winners and Losers in Russia's Economic Transition." *The American Economic Review* 88(5): 1094–1116.

Bräutigam, Deborah. 2000. *Aid Dependence and Governance*. Stockholm: Almqvist & Wiksell International.

Bräutigam, Deborah and Kwesi Botchwey. 1992. "The Institutional Impact of Aid Dependence on Recipients in Africa." Working Paper 1999:2. Chr. Michelsen Institute, Bergen.

Brennan, Geoffrey and James M. Buchanan. 1985. *The Reason of Rules: Constitutional Political Economy*. Cambridge: Cambridge University Press.

Bromley, Daniel W., David Feeny, Margaret McKean, Pauline Peters, Jere Gilles, Ronald Oakerson, C. Ford Runge, and James Thomson, eds. 1992. *Making the Commons Work: Theory, Practice, and Policy*. San Francisco, CA: ICS Press.

Browne, Stephen. 1997. "Beyond Aid: Redefining Development Cooperation." Public Lecture, World Institute for Development Economics and Research. Helsinki, April 29.

———. 1999. *Beyond Aid: From Patronage to Partnership*. Aldershot: Ashgate Publishing Co.

Browne, Stephen and C. Pflaumer. 1996. "Aiding the Triple Transition in Ukraine." *The International Journal of Technical Cooperation* 2(1): 74–87.

Brunetti, Aymo and Beatrice Weder. 1994. "Political Credibility and Economic Growth in Less Developed Countries." *Constitutional Political Economy* 5(1): 23–43.

Buchanan, James M. 1960. *Fiscal Theory and Political Economy*. Chapel Hill: University of North Carolina Press.

———. 1975. *The Limits of Liberty Between Anarchy and Leviathan*. Indianapolis: Liberty Fund.

———. 1986. *Liberty, Market, and State—Political Economy in the 1980's*. New York: New York University Press.

———. 1987. *Public Finance in Democratic Process, Fiscal Institutions, and Individual Choice*. Chapel Hill: University of North Carolina Press.

———. 1988. "Contractarian Political Economy and Constitutional Interpretation." *The American Economic Review* 78(2): 135–139.

———. 1989a. *Essays on the Political Economy*. Honolulu: University of Hawaii Press.

———. 1989b. "The Achievement and Limits of Public Choice in Diagnosing Government Failure and in Offering Bases for Constructive Reform." In R.D. Tollison and V.J. Vanberg, eds. *Explorations into Constitutional Economics*. College Station, TX: A&M University Press.

———. 1991. *The Economics and Ethics of Constitutional Order*. Ann Arbor: University of Michigan Press.

———. 1996. "The Domain of Constitutional Economics." *Constitutional Political Economy* 1(1): 1–18.

———. 1999. *Public Finance in the Democratic Process, Fiscal Institutions, and Individual Choice*. Indianapolis: Liberty Fund, Inc.

———. 2004. "The Status of the Status Quo." *Constitutional Political Economy* 15: 133–144.

Buchanan, James M. and Gordon Tullock. 1962. *The Calculus of Consent*. Ann Arbor: University of Michigan Press.

Buchanan, James M. and Richard E. Wagner. 1977. *Democracy in Deficit: The Political Legacy of Lord Keynes*. New York: Academic Press.

Buchanan, James M. and Viktor Vanberg. 1989. "Interests and Theories in Constitutional Choice." *Journal of Theoretical Politics* 1: 49–62.

Burnside, Craig and David Dollar. 2000a. "Aid Policies and Growth." *American Economic Review* 90(4): 847–868.

———. 2000b. "Aid, Growth, the Incentive Regime, and Poverty Reduction." In Christopher L. Gilbert and David Vines, eds. *The World Bank: Structure and Policies.* 210–227. Cambridge: Cambridge University Press.

Campbell, Donald E. 1995. *Incentives: Motivations and the Economics of Information.* Cambridge, UK: Cambridge University Press.

Campos, Ed and Sanjay Pradhan. 1996. "Budgetary Institutions and Expenditure Outcomes: Binding Governments to Fiscal Performance." Policy Research Working Paper no. 1646. Washington, DC: World Bank.

Cairncross, Alec. 1985. "Economics in Theory and Practice." *American Economic Review* 75(2): 1–14.

Catterson, Julie and Claes Lindahl. 1999. *The Sustainability Enigma: Aid Dependency and the Phasing Out of Projects—The Case of Swedish Aid to Tanzania.* Stockholm: Almqvist and Wiksell International.

Center for Global Development. 2004. *On the Brink: Weak States and US National Security.* Washington, DC: CDG.

Cerf, Vinton and Robert Kahn. 1974. "A Protocol for Packet Network Intercommunication." *IEEE Transactions and Communications* COM-22, No. 5: 637–648.

Cernea, Michael. 1987. "Farmer Organization and Institutional Building for Sustainable Development." *Regional Development Dialog* 8(2): 1–24.

Cheema, G.S. and D.A. Rondinelli. 1983. *Decentralization and Development: Policy Implementation in Developing Countries.* Beverly Hills, CA: Sage Publications.

Chenery, Hollis. 1971. *Studies in Development Planning.* Cambridge, MA: Harvard University Press.

Chenery, Hollis and Alan M. Strout. 1966. "Foreign Assistance and Economic Development." *American Economic Review* 56(4): 679–733.

Ciolek, Matthew. 2003. "Internet Structure and Development: on strategic uses of the archetypes of the networked mind." Accessed at http://www.ciolek.com/PAPERS/pnc-taipei-99.html.

Collier, Paul. 1997. "The Failure of Conditionality," in Catherine Gwin and Joan Nelson, eds. *Perspectives on Aid and Development.* Baltimore: Johns Hopkins University Press.

———. 1999. "Consensus-Building, Knowledge, and Conditionality." Paper presented to the International Symposium on Global Finance and Development, Tokyo, Japan.

Collier, Paul and J.W. Gunning. 1999. "Why has Africa Grown Slowly?" *Journal of Economic Perspectives* 13(3): 3–22.

Commons, John R. 1931. "Institutional Economics." *The American Economic Review* 21(4): 648–657.

Conquest, Robert. 1986. *The Harvest of Sorrow: Soviet Collectivization and the Terror-Famine.* New York: Oxford University Press.

Cooper, Fredrick and Randall Packard. 1997. *International Development and the Social Sciences: Essays on the History and Politics of Knowledge*. Berkeley: University of California Press.

Cowen, Tyler. 1997. *The Theory of Market Failure*. Fairfax, VA: George Mason University Press.

Crawford, Sue E.S. and Elinor Ostrom. 1995. "A Grammar of Institutions." *American Political Science Review* 89(3) (September): 582–600.

Daniloff, Miranda. 2000. "Singapore Leader Outlines Lessons of Leadership." Kennedy School of Government *News Focus* October 17.

Demsetz, Harold. 1996. "The Core Disagreement between Pigou, the Profession, and Coase, in the Analysis of the Externality Question." *European Journal of Political Economy* Vol. 12(4): 565–579.

de Soto, Hernando. 2000. *The Mystery of Capital: Why Capitalism Triumphs in the West and Fails Everywhere Else*. New York: Basic Books.

Devarajan, Shantayanan, David Dollar, and Torgny Holmgren, eds. 2001. *Aid and Reform in Africa: A Report from Ten Countries*. Washington, DC: World Bank.

Devarajan, Shantayanan and Vinaya Swaroop. 1998. "The Implications of Foreign Aid Fungibility for Development Assistance." Policy Research Working Paper. Washington, DC: World Bank.

Dewey, John. 1982. *The Middle Works 1899–1924, Vol. 12: Reconstruction in Philosophy and Essays*. Carbondale: Southern Illinois University Press.

Diamond, Larry, Jonathan Hartlyn, Juan J. Linz, and Seymour Martin Lipset, eds. 1999. *Democracy in Developing Countries: Latin America*. 2nd ed. Boulder, CO: Lynne Rienner Publishers.

Dietz, Thomas, Elinor Ostrom, and Paul Stern. 2003. "The Struggle to Govern the Commons." *Science* 302 (December 12): 1907–1912.

Doel, Hans Van Den. 1979. *Democracy and Welfare Economics*. Cambridge: Cambridge University Press.

Dollar, David and Jakob Svensson. 2000. "What Explains the Success or Failure of Structural Adjustment Programmes?" *Economic Journal* 110 (October): 894–917.

Dollar, David and William Easterly. 1999. "The Search for the Key: Aid, Investment, and Policies in Africa." Policy Research Working Paper 2070, Washington, DC: World Bank.

Domar, Evsey. 1957. *Essays in the Theory of Economic Growth*. Westport, CT: Greenwood.

Doornbos, Martin. 2001. "Good Governance: The Rise and Decline of a Policy Metaphor?" *Journal of Development Studies* 37(6): 93–108.

———. 2003. "Good Governance: The Metamorphosis of a Policy Metaphor." *Journal of International Affairs* 57(1): 3–18.

Dunbar, Judith. 2004. "Ubudehe and the Kecamatan Development Projects: Case Study and Comparative Analysis." Master of Arts in Law and Diplomacy Thesis, The Fletcher School, Tufts University.

Easterly, William. 1999. "The Ghost of Financing Gap: Testing the Growth Model Used in the International Financial Institutions." *Journal of Development Economics* 60: 423–438.

———. 2001. *The Elusive Quest for Growth: Economists' Misadventures in the Tropics.* Cambridge, MA: MIT Press.

———. 2002a. "The Cartel of Good Intentions: The Problem of Bureaucracy in Foreign Aid." *Policy Reform* 5(4): 223–250.

———. 2002b. "What Did Structural Adjustment Adjust?: The Association of Policies and Growth with Repeated IMF and World Bank Adjustment Loans." Working Paper no. 11. Washington, DC: Institute for International Economics, Center for Global Development.

———. 2003. "Can Foreign Aid Buy Growth?" *Journal of Economic Perspectives* 17(3) (Summer): 23–48.

The Economist. 1998. "Ivan of All Trades." November 5.

———. 2003. "The Whiff of Rotting Tyranny." January 16.

Edgren, Gus. 1995. "Indo-Swedish Development Cooperation: Objective, Issues and Achievements." In V. Sahai, ed. *Sharing Challenges: The Indo-Swedish Development Cooperation Programme.* 8–46. Stockholm: Ministry for Foreign Affairs.

Eizenstat, Stuart, John E. Porter, and Jeremy M. Weinstein. 2005. "Rebuilding Weak States." *Foreign Affairs* 84(1): 134–146.

Elazar, Daniel. 1988. *The American Constitutional Tradition.* Lincoln: University of Nebraska Press.

———. 1995. *Covenant and Polity: Vol. I Covenant and Polity in Biblical Israel, Vol. 2 Covenant, and Commonwealth: The Western Covenantal Tradition; Vol. 3 Covenant and Constitutionalism: Modern Covenants and the New Science of Politics, Vol. 4 Covenant and Civil Society.* New Brunswick, NJ: Transaction Publishers.

Eriksson Skoog, Gun. 2000. *The Soft Budget Constraint: The Emergence, Persistence and Logic of an Institution.* Dordrecht, Netherlands: Kluwer.

Elgström, Ole. 1992. *Foreign Aid Negotiations.* Aldershot, England: Avebury.

Elman, J.L. 1993. "Learning and Development in Neural Networks: The Importance of Starting Small." *Cognition* 48: 71–99.

Escobar, Arturo. 1996. *Encountering Development.* Princeton Paperbacks.

Eucken, Walter. 1952. *Grundsatze der Wirtschaftspolitik.* Tubingen: JCB Mohr.

———. 1992. *The Foundations of Economics: History and Theory in the Analysis of Economic Reality.* Berlin: Springer Verlag.

Evans, J.St. B.T. 1993. "Bias and Rationality." In K.I. Manktelow and D.E. Over, eds. *Rationality, Psychological and Philosophical Perspectives.* London and New York: Routledge.

Farazmand, Ali. 2001. *Handbook of Comparative and Development Public Administration.* New York: Marcel Dekker.

Felser, James W. 1982. *American Public Administration: Patterns of the Past.* Washington, DC: American Society for Public Administration.

Feyzioglu, Tarhan, Vinaya Swaroop, and Min Zhu. 1998. "A Panel Data Analysis of the Fungibility of Foreign Aid." *World Bank Economic Review* 12(1): 29–58.

Friedman, Milton. 1953. *Essays in Positive Economics*. Chicago: University of Chicago Press.

———. 1999. "John Maynard Keynes." *The Laissez Faire City Times* 3(10) (March 8).

Fuster, Joaquin. 1995. *Memory in the Cerebral Cortex: An Empirical Approach to Neural Networks in the Human and Nonhuman Primate*. Cambridge: MIT Press.

Gambetta, Diego. 1993. *The Sicilian Mafia: The Business of Private Protection*. Cambridge, MA: Harvard University Press.

Gellar, Sheldon. 2005. *Democracy in Senegal; Tocquevillian Analytics in Africa* New York: Palgrave Macmillan.

Gellner, Ernest. 1991. "Civil Society in Historical Context." *International Social Science Journal* 43(129): 495–510.

Gibson, Clark and Matthew Hoffmann. 2005. "Making Democrats of Dictators: Foreign Aid and Africa's Political Liberalization." Working Paper. San Diego: University of California.

Gibson, Clark, Margaret McKean, and Elinor Ostrom, eds. 2000. *People and Forests: Communities, Institutions, and Governance*. Cambridge, MA: MIT Press.

Gibson, Clark, Krister Andersson, Elinor Ostrom, and Sujai Shivakumar. 2005. *The Samaritan's Dilemma: The Political Economy of Development Assistance*. Oxford: Oxford University Press.

Gilbert, Christopher C., Andrew Powell, and David Vines. 1999. "Positioning the World Bank." *Economic Journal* 109(459): 598–633.

Goldschmidt-Clermont, Louisella. 2000. "Measuring and Valuing Non SNA Economic Activities." *Handbook of National Accounting Series* F, 75(2): 73–111. New York: United Nations.

Gordon, Scott. 1999. *Controlling the State, Constitutionalism from Ancient Athens to Today*. Cambridge, MA: Harvard University Press.

Government of Rwanda. 2004. "Ubudehe to Fight Poverty." Ministry of Local Government and Social Affairs (MINALOC) and the National Poverty Reduction Programme (NPRP) at Ministry of Finance and Economic Planning.

Grossman, Sanford and Oliver Hart. 1986. "The Costs and Benefits of Ownership: A Theory of Vertical and Lateral Integration." *Journal of Political Economy* 94: 691–719.

Hamilton, Alexander, James Madison, and John Jay. 1788 (rpt. 1987.) *The Federalist Papers*. New York: Penguin Books.

Hansen, Henrik and Finn Tarp. 2000. "Aid Effectiveness Disputed." *Journal of International Development* 13(3) (April): 375–398.

———. 2001. "Aid and Growth Regressions." *Journal of Development Economics* 64(2): 547–570.

Haq, Mahbub ul. 1972. "Employment and Income Distribution in the 1970s: A New Perspective." *Development Digest*.

Hardin, Garrett. 1968. "The Tragedy of the Commons." *Science* 162: 1243–1248.

Hayek, Freidrick A. 1937. "Presidential Address Delivered Before the London Economic Club; November 10 1936." *Economica* 4: 35.

———. 1944. *The Road to Serfdom.* Chicago: University of Chicago Press.

———. 1945. Use of Knowledge in Society. *American Economic Review* 35(4): 519–530.

———. 1948. *Individualism and Economic Order.* Chicago: University of Chicago Press.

———. 1952a. *The Sensory Order, An Inquiry into the Foundations of Theoretical Psychology.* Chicago: University of Chicago Press.

———. 1952b. "Scientism and the Study of Society." In Fritz Machlup, ed. *Essays on Hayek.* New York: New York University Press.

———. 1960. *The Constitution of Liberty,* Chicago: University of Chicago Press.

———. 1976. *Law, Legislation and Liberty, Vol. 2: The Mirage of Social Justice.* Chicago: University of Chicago Press.

———. 1978. *New Studies in Philosophy, Politics, Economics, and the History of Ideas.* Chicago: The University of Chicago Press.

Heady, Ferrel. 2001. *Public Administration: A Comparative Perspective.* (6th ed.) New York: Marcel Dekker, Inc.

Hicks, Ursula. 1961. *Development from Below.* Oxford: Oxford University Press.

Hilton, Rita M. 2002. "Institutional Incentives for Resource Mobilization in Farmer-Managed and Agency-Managed Irrigation Systems." In Ganesh P. Shivakoti and Elinor Ostrom, eds. *Improving Irrigation Governance and Management in Nepal.* 150–176. Oakland, CA: ICS Press.

Hobbes, Thomas. 1960. *Leviathan or the Matter, Forme, and Power of a Commonwealth Ecclesiasticall and Civill.* Oxford: Blackwell.

———. 1972. *Man and Citizen, Thomas Hobbes's De Homine.* New York: Doubleday.

Hodge, Graeme A. 2002. "Good Governance and the Privatizing State: Some International Lessons." *Journal of Economic & Social Policy* 6(2): 56–67.

Holland, J.H., K.J. Holyoak, R.W. Nisbitt, and P.R. Thagard. 1986. *Induction: Processes of Inference, Learning and Discovery.* Cambridge, MA: The MIT Press.

Holmstrom, Bengt. 1982a. *Essays in Economics and Management in Honor of Lars Wahlbeck.* Stockholm. Swedish School of Economics.

———. 1982b. "Moral Hazard in Teams." *Bell Journal of Economics* 13 (Autumn): 324–340.

Holmstrom, Bengt and Paul R. Milgrom. 1991. "Multi-Task Principal Agent Analyses: Incentive Contracts, Asset Ownership and Job Design." *Journal of Law Economics and Organization* 7 (Spring): 24–52.

Hume, David. 1966. *An Enquiry Concerning the Principles of Morals.* Chicago: Open Court Publishing Co.

———. 1975. *Treatise on Human Nature.* London: Oxford University Press.

———. 1999. *An Enquiry Concerning Human Understanding.* Oxford: Oxford University Press.

Huntington, Samuel P. and Myron Weiner, eds. 1987. *Understanding Political Development.* Boston, MA: Little, Brown.

Hutt, William H. 1940. "The Concept of Consumers' Sovereignty." *Economic Journal* 50: 66–77.

Israel, Arturo. 1987. *Institutional Development*. Washington, DC: The World Bank.

Johnson, John H. and Sulaiman S. Wasty. 1993. "Borrower Ownership of Adjustment Programs and the Political Economy of Reform." Discussion Paper no. 199. Washington, DC: World Bank.

Jones, Philip R. 1995. "Rents from In-Kind Subsidy: 'Charity' in the Public Sector." *Public Choice* 86 (3–4).

Kaufmann, D., A. Kraay, and P. Zoido-Lobatón. 1999. "Governance Matters." World Bank Policy Research Working Paper 2196.

Kilby, Christopher. 1999. "Aid and Sovereignty." *Social Theory and Practice* 25(11): 79–92.

Killick, Tony. 1995. *The Flexible Economy: Causes and Consequences of the Adaptability of National Economies*. London: Routledge.

Kiser, Larry and Elinor Ostrom. 1982. "The Three Worlds of Action: A Metatheoretical Synthesis of Institutional Approaches." In Elinor Ostrom, ed. *Strategies of Political Inquiry*. 179–222. Beverly Hills, CA: Sage.

Klein, Daniel B. 1997. "Convention, Social Order, and the Two Coordinations." *Constitutional Political Economy* 8: 91–106.

Klein, Lawrence R. 1980. *The Keynesian Revolution*. London: Macmillan.

Knowles, L.C.A. 1936. *The Economic Development of the British Overseas Empire*. London: Routledge.

Krueger, Anne O. 1974. "The Political Economy of the Rent Seeking Society." *American Economic Review* 64(3): 291–303.

———. 1990. "Government Failures in Development." *The Journal of Economic Perspectives* 4(3): 9–23.

———. 1998. "Wither the World Bank and the IMF?" *Journal of Economic Literature* 36(4): 1983–2020.

Krueger, Anne O., Constantine Michalopoulos, and Vernon Ruttan, eds. 1989. *Aid and Development*. Baltimore, MD: Johns Hopkins University Press.

Kuznets, Simon. 1956. *Economic Development and Cultural Change*. Chicago: University of Chicago Press.

———. 1971. *Economic Growth of Nations: Total Output and Production Structure*. Cambridge: Harvard University Press.

Kuhnert, Stephan. 2001. "An Evolutionary Theory of Collective Action, Schumpeterian Entrepreneurship for the Common Good." *Constitutional Political Economy* 12(1): 13–29.

Lachmann, Ludwig. 1971. *The Legacy of Max Weber*. Berkeley, CA: University of California Press.

———. 1978. *Capital and its Structure*. Kansas City: Sheed, Andrews and McMeel.

Lakatoš, Imre. 1970. "Falsification and the Methodology of Scientific Research Programs." In I. Lakatoš and A. Musgrave, eds. *Criticism and the Growth of Knowledge*. Cambridge: University Press Cambridge.

Lal, Deepak. 1983. *The Poverty of "Development Economics."* London: Institute of Economic Affairs.

———. 2000. "Globalization, Imperialism and Regulation." Department of Economics Working Paper: 810. University of California, Los Angeles.

Lam, Wai Fung. 1998. *Governing Irrigation Systems in Nepal.* San Francisco, CA: ICS Press.

Langlois, Richard. 1986. "The New Institutional Economics: An Introductory Essay." In R.N. Langlois, ed. *Economics as a Process, Essays in New Institutional Economics.* Cambridge: Cambridge University Press.

Landell-Mills, Pierre and Ismail Serageldin. 1991. "Governance and the Development Process." *Finance & Development* Vol. 28(3): 14–17.

Lasswell, Harold D. and Abraham Kaplan. 1950. *Power and Society: A Framework for Political Inquiry.* New Haven: Yale University Press.

Lavoie, Don. 1985. *National Economic Planning: What is Left?* Washington, DC: Cato Institute.

Leftwich, Alan. 1994. "Governance, the State, and the Politics of Development." *Development and Change* 25(2): 363–386.

Leontief, Wassily. 1982. "What Hope for the Economy." *New York Review of Books*, August 12.

———. 1986. *Input-Output Economics.* Oxford: Oxford University Press.

Levi, Margaret. 2002. "The State of the Study of the State." In Ira Katznelson and Helen V. Milner, eds. *Political Science—State of the Discipline.* New York: W.W. Norton & Co.

Levy, Victor. 1987. "Anticipated Development Assistance, Temporary Relief Aid, and Consumption Behavior of Low-Income Countries." *The Economic Journal* 97(386): 446–458.

Lewis, W. Arthur. 1954. "Economic Development with Unlimited Supplies of Labor." *Manchester School* 22: 139–191.

Lewis, Ioan M. 1961. *A Pastoral Democracy.* New York: Africana Publishing.

———. 1994. *Blood and Bone: The Call of Kinship in Somali Society.* Trenton, NJ: Red Sea Press.

Leys, Colin. 1995. *The Rise and Fall of Development Theory.* London: James Currey Ltd.

Lipset, Seymour Martin. 1959. "Some Social Requisites of Democracy: Economic Development and Political Legitimacy." *American Political Science Review* 53(1): 69–105.

Little, I.M.D. 1982. *Economic Development.* New York: Basic Books.

Lyons, Terrence and Ahmed I. Samatar, 1995. *Somalia: State Collapse, Multilateral Intervention, and Strategies for Political Reconstruction.* Washington, DC: Brookings.

Mahoney, Michael and Walter Weimer. 1994. "Friedrich A. Hayek (1989–1992)." *American Psychologist* 49(1): 63.

Maipose, Gervase, Gloria Somolekae, and Timothy Johnston. 1997. "Effective Aid Management: The Case of Botswana." In Jerker Carlsson, Gloria Somolekae, and Nicholas van de Walle, eds. *Foreign Aid in Africa: Learning from Country Experiences.* 16–35. Uppsala: Nordic Africa Institute.

Maizels, Alfred and Machiko Nissanke. 1984. "Motivations for Aid to Developing Countries." *World Development* 12(9): 879–900.

Mamdani, Mahmood. 2002. *When Victims Become Killers: Colonialism, Nativism, and the Genocide in Rwanda.* Princeton: Princeton University Press.

Martens, Bertin. 2000. "The Institutional Economics of Foreign Aid. How Donor Country Aid Institutions, Rather than Beneficiary Country Policies, Affect the Performance of Foreign Aid Programmes." Paper presented for the Annual Conference of the International Society for New Institution Economics (ISNIE), Tübingen, Germany, September, 22–24.

Martens, Bertin, Uwe Mummert, Peter Murrell, and Paul Seabright. 2002. *The Institutional Economics of Foreign Aid.* Cambridge, UK: Cambridge University Press.

Mathur, Kuldeep. 2001. "Good Governance State and Democracy." Paper presented at the Conference on Beyond the Post-Washington Consensus, Governance and the Public Domain in Contrasting Economies—the cases of India and Canada.

Mayr, Ernst. 1982. *The Growth of Biological Thought.* Cambridge: Harvard University Press.

Mbaku, J.M. 1998. "Constitutional Engineering and the Transition to Democracy in Post-Cold War Africa." *The Independent Review* 2(4): 501–517.

———. 2003. "Minority Rights in Plural Societies." Accessed at http://www.india-seminar.com/2000/490/490%20mbaku.htm.

McCay, Bonnie J. and James Acheson, eds. 1987. *The Question of the Commons: The Culture and Ecology of Communal Resources.* Tucson: University of Arizona Press.

McCloskey, Deirdre N. 1988. "The Rhetoric of Economic Development." *Cato Journal* 7(1): 249–254.

———. 1997. *The Rhetoric of Economics.* Madison: University of Wisconsin Press.

McGinnis, Michael D., ed. 1999a. *Polycentric Governance and Development: Readings from the Workshop in Political Theory and Policy Analysis.* Ann Arbor: University of Michigan Press.

———. 1999b. *Polycentricity and Local Public Economies: Readings from the Workshop in Political Theory and Policy Analysis.* Ann Arbor: University of Michigan Press.

———. 2000. *Polycentric Games and Institutions: Readings from the Workshop in Political Theory and Policy Analysis.* Ann Arbor: University of Michigan Press.

McGow, Lisa. 1995. "The Ignored Cost of Adjustment: Women Under SAPs in Africa." Paper prepared for the Fourth United Nations Conference on Women, Beijing, China.

McGuire, Martin and Mancur Olson. 1996. "The Economics of Autocracy and Majority Rule: The Invisible Hand and the Use of Force." *Journal of Economic Literature* 34: 72–96.

Meier, Gerald M. 1995. *Leading Issues in Economic Development.* 6th ed. New York: Oxford University Press.

Menger, Carl. 1984. *Principles of Economics.* Libertarian Press.

Milgrom, Paul and John Roberts. 1992. *Economics, Organization and Management.* Englewood Cliffs, NJ: Prentice Hall.

Miller, Gary. 1992. *Managerial Dilemmas: The Political Economy of Hierarchy*. New York: Cambridge University Press.

Mirowski, Phillip. 1992. *More Heat than Light, Economics as Social Physics, Physics as Nature's Economics*. Cambridge: Cambridge University Press.

Mises, Ludwig von. 1966. *Human Action: A Treatise in Economics*. Chicago: Contemporary Books.

Montesquieu, Charles de Secondat, Baron de. 1989. *Spirit of the Laws*. Cambridge: Cambridge University Press.

Morss, Elliott R. 1984. "Institutional Destruction Resulting from Donor and Project Proliferation in Sub-Saharan African Countries." *World Development* 12(4): 465–470.

Mosely, Paul. 1987. *Foreign Aid: Its Defense and Reform*. Lexington: University of Kentucky Press.

Müller-Armack, Alfred. 1989. "The Meaning of the Social Market Economy." In A. Peacock and H. Willgerodt, eds. *Germany's Social Market Economy*: 82–86.

Nayar, Baldev Raj. 1972. *The Modernization Imperative and Indian Planning*. Delhi: Vikas.

———. 1997. "Nationalist Planning for Autarky and State Hegemony: Development Strategy Under Nehru." *Indian Economic Review* 32(1): 13–38.

National Research Council. 2002. *The Drama of the Commons*. Washington, DC: National Academies Press.

Nelson, Michael and Ram D. Singh. 1998. "Democracy, Political Freedom, Fiscal Policy, and Growth in LDCs: A Fresh Look." *Economic Development and Cultural Change* 46(4): 677–696.

New York Times. 2000. "In Report, Anan Sketches Future Path of U.N." April 3.

Newell, Alan and H.A. Simon. 1972. *Human Problem Solving*. Englewood Cliffs, NJ: Prentice Hall.

Ngaido, Tidiane and Michael Kirk. 2001. "Collective Action, Property Rights and Devolution of Rangeland Management: Selected Examples from Africa and Asia." In Ruth Meinzen-Dick, Anna Knox, and Monica Di Gregorio, eds. *Collective Action, Property Rights and Devolution of Natural Resource Management*. Feldafing, Germany: Deutsche Stiftung für Ernährun and Landwirtschaft.

Niskanen, William. 1986. "Economists and Politicians." *Journal of Policy Analysis and Management* 2: 234–244.

———. 1998. *Policy Analysis and Public Choice*. Cheltenham, UK: Edward Elgar.

North, Douglass C. 1990. *Institutions, Institutional Change, and Economic Performance*. Cambridge: Cambridge University Press.

———. 1994. "Economic Performance Through Time." *American Economics Review* 84: 359–368.

———. 2005. *Understanding the Process of Economic Change*. Princeton, NJ: Princeton University Press.

Nurske, Ragnar. 1953. *Problems of Capital-Formation in Underdeveloped Countries*. Oxford: Basil Blackwell.

Oakerson, Ronald J. 1992. "Analyzing the Commons: A Framework." In Daniel W. Bromley et al., eds. *Making the Commons Work: Theory, Practice, and Policy*. 41–59. San Francisco, CA: ICS Press.

OECD (Organisation for Economic Co-operation and Development). 1992. *DAC Principles for Effective Aid*. Paris: OECD, Development Assistance Committee.

———. 2001. "Investing in Development." *OECD Observer*. Paris: OECD.

Olowu, C.A.B. 1999. "Stalled Decentralization Reforms: The Nigerian Case and Lessons for Other Countries." In E.H. Valsan, ed. *Democracy, Decentralization and Development: Selected International Experiences*. Brussels: International Association of Schools and Institute: 21–29.

Olowu, Dele and Wunsch, James S. 1995. *The Failure of the Centralized State: Institutions and Self-governance in Africa*. San Francisco: ICS Press.

Olson, Mancur. 1965. *The Logic of Collective Action*. Cambridge, MA: Harvard University Press.

Ophulus, W. 1973. "Leviathan or Oblivion." In H.E. Daly, ed. *Toward a Steady State Economy*. Newyork: Freeman Press.

Ostrom, Elinor. 1990. *Governing the Commons: The Evolution of Institutions for Collective Action*. Cambridge: Cambridge University Press.

———. 1996. "Incentives, Rules of the Game, and Development." In *Proceedings of the Annual World Bank Conference on Development Economics 1995*. 207–234. Washington, DC: The World Bank.

———. 1997. "The Comparative Study of Public Economies." Acceptance Paper for the Frank E. Seidman Distinguished Award in Political Economy.

———. 1998. "A Behavioral Approach to the Rational Choice Theory of Collective Action." *American Political Science Review* 92(1): 1–22.

———. 1999a. "Social Capital, A Fad or Fundamental Concept." In Partha Dasgupta and Ismail Serageldin, eds. *Social Capital: A Multifaceted Perspective*. Washington, DC: World Bank.

———. 1999b. "Institutional Rational Choice: An Assessment of the Institutional Analysis and Development Framework." In P.A. Sabatier, ed. *Theories of the Policy Process*. Boulder, CO: Westview Press.

———. 2000. "Radical Decentralization in Developing Countries; A Recommended Panacea without Empirically Grounded Institutional Theory." Paper prepared for the Symposium on Development and the Nation State. St. Louis: Washington University.

———. 2005. *Understanding Institutional Diversity*. Princeton: Princeton University Press.

Ostrom, Elinor and Roy Gardner. 1993. "Coping with Asymmetries in the Commons: Self-Governing Irrigation Systems Can Work." *Journal of Economic Perspectives* 7(4) (Fall): 93–112.

Ostrom, Elinor, Larry Schoreder, and Susan Wynne. 1993. *Institutional Incentives and Sustainable Development: Infrastructure Policies in Perspective*. Boulder CO: Westview Press.

Ostrom, Elinor, Roy Gardner, and James M. Walker. 1994. *Rules, Games, and Common-Pool Resources*. Ann Arbor: University of Michigan Press.

Ostrom, Elinor, Clark Gibson, Sujai Shivakumar, and Krister Andersson, 2002. *Aid, Incentives, and Sustainability; An Institutional Analysis of Development Cooperation*. Stockholm: Sida.

Ostrom, Vincent. 1971. *The Political Theory of a Compound Republic: Designing the American Experiment*. 2d rev. ed. San Francisco: Institute for Contemporary Studies Press.

———. 1973. *The Intellectual Crisis in American Public Administration*. Tuscaloosa: University of Alabama Press.

———. 1991. *The Meaning of American Federalism*. San Francisco: ICS Press.

———. 1997. *The Meaning of Democracy and the Vulnerability of Democracies, A Response to Tocqueville's Challenge*. Ann Arbor: University of Michigan Press.

———. 1999. "Polycentricity." (Parts 1 and 2) In Michael D. McGinnis, ed. *Polycentricity and Local Public Economies*. Ann Arbor: University of Michigan Press.

Ostrom, Vincent and Elinor Ostrom. 1977. "Public Goods and Public Choices." In E.S. Savas, ed. *Alternatives for Delivering Public Services: Toward Improved Performance*. 7–49 Boulder, CO.: Westview Press.

Ostrom, Vincent, D. Feeny, and H. Picht, eds. 1988. *Rethinking Institutional Analysis and Development: Issues, Alternatives, and Choices*. San Francisco: ICS Press.

Ostrom, Vincent, Robert Warren, and Charles M. Tiebout. 1961. "The Organization of Government in Metropolitan Areas: A Theoretical Inquiry." *American Political Science Review* 55: 831–842.

Pack, Howard and Janet Rothenberg Pack. 1990. "Is Foreign Aid Fungible? The Case of Indonesia." *Economic Journal* 100(399) (March): 188–194.

Polanyi, Michael. 1951. *The Logic of Liberty*, Chicago: University of Chicago Press.

Pollitt, Michael G. and Andrew S.J. Smith. 2001. "The Restructuring and Privatization of British Rail, Was it Really that Bad?" University of Cambridge, DAE Working Paper: 0118: 30.

Popper, Karl. 1971. *The Open Society and its Enemies. Vol. I*. Princeton Paperbacks.

———. 1972. *Objective Knowledge*. Oxford: Oxford University Press.

———. 2001. *All Life is Problem Solving*. London: Routledge.

Pourgerami, Abbas. 1998. "The Political Economy of Development; A Cross-National Test of Development-Democracy Growth Hypothesis." *Public Choice* 58(2): 123–141.

Prebisch, Raul. 1970. *Change and Development: Latin America's Great Task*. Washington, DC: Inter-American Development Bank.

Rasmusen, Eric. 1989. *Games and Information: An Introduction to Game Theory*. Oxford: Basil Blackwell.

Rivera-Batiz, Francisco L. 2000. "Foreign Direct Investment in Latin America, Current Trends and Future Prospects, Interregional Investment in Trade and Cooperation: Asia—Latin America." *ESCAP Studies in Trade and Investment* 43. Bangkok: ESCAP.

Rizzello, Salvatore and Margherita Turvani. 2000. "Institutions Meet Mind: The Way Out of an Impasse." *Constitutional Political Economy* 11(2): 165–80.

Robbins, Lionel. 1932. *The Nature and Significance of Economic Science.* London: Macmillan.

Roberts, John. 1979. "Incentives in Planning Procedures for the Provision of Public Goods." *Review of Economic Studies* 46: 283–292.

Rosenstein-Rodan, Paul. 1943. "Problems of Industrialization in Eastern and Southeastern Europe." *Economic Journal* 53: 202–213.

Rostow, Walt W. 1960. *The Stages of Economic Growth.* Cambridge: Cambridge University Press.

———. 1969. *Economics of Take Off into Sustainable Growth.* London: Palgrave Macmillan.

Sabetti, Filippo. 2002. *The Search for Good Government, Understanding the Paradox of Italian Democracy.* Montreal: McGill-Queens University Press.

———. 2004a. "Local Roots of Constitutionalism." *Perspectives on Political Science* 33(2): 70–78.

———. 2004b. "Is a Strong Central State Necessary for Democratic Development?" Working Paper, Department of Political Science, McGill University.

Samuelson, Paul. 1948. "Consumption Theory in terms of Revealed Preference," *Econometrica* 15: 243–253.

———. 1954. "The Pure Theory of Public Expenditure." *Rev. Econ. Stat.* 36: 378–389.

Sawyer, Amos. 2005. *Beyond Plunder: Toward Democratic Governance in Liberia.* Boulder CO: Lynne Rienner Publishers.

Schleifer, Andrei and Daniel Triesman. 1999. *The Economics and Politics of Transition to an Open Market Economy: Russia.* Paris: OECD.

Schumpeter, Joseph A. 1911. *The Theory of Economic Development: An Inquiry into Profits, Capital, Credit, Interest and the Business Cycle.* 1934 translation. Cambridge, MA: Harvard University Press.

———. 1947. *Capitalism, Socialism and Democracy.* New York: Harper & Brothers.

Scopino, A.J. 1997. *The Progressive Movement, 1900–1917.* Carlisle, MA: Discovery Books.

Scott, J.C. 1998. *Seeing Like a State: How Certain Schemes to Improve the Human Condition Have Failed.* New Haven and London: Yale University Press.

Seabright, Paul. 2002. "Conflicts of Objectives and Task Allocation in Aid Agencies." In Bertin Martens, Uwe Mummert, Peter Murrell, and Paul Seabright, eds. *The Institutional Economics of Foreign Aid.* Cambridge: Cambridge University Press.

Seers, Douglas. 1969. "The Meaning of Development." *International Development Review* 11(4): 2–6.

Sen, Amartya K. 1999a. *Development as Freedom.* Oxford: Oxford University Press.

———. 1999b. *Commodities and Capabilities.* New Delhi: Oxford University Press.

Shackle G.L.S. 1967. *The Years of High Theory: Invention and Tradition in Economic thought, 1926–1939.* Cambridge: Cambridge University Press.

Shivakumar, Sujai J. 2000. "Valuation as an Issue in National Accounting and Policy Analysis." *Handbook of National Accounting Series* F, 75(2): 147–178. New York: United Nations.

Shivakumar, Sujai J. 2003. "The Place of Indigenous Institutions in Constitutional Order." *Constitutional Political Economy* 14(1): 3–22.

Sidgwick, H. 1973. *The Methods of Ethics*. 7th ed. London: Macmillan.

Simon, Herbert A. 1962. "The Architecture of Complexity." *Proceedings of the American Philosophical Society* 106(6): 467–482.

———. 1986. "Interview with Herbert A. Simon." In B.J. Baars, ed. *The Cognitive Revolution in Psychology*. New York: Guilford Press: 362.

———. 1987. "Rationality in Psychology and Economics." In Robin M. Hogarth and Melvin W. Reder, eds. *Rational choice: The Contrast Between Economics and Psychology*. Chicago: University of Chicago Press.

———. 1995. "The Information Processing Theory of Mind." *American Psychologist* 50(7): 507–508.

Skidelsky, Robert. 2001. *John Maynard Keynes: Fighting for Britain, 1937–1946*. New York: Viking Press.

Slater, John. 1974. *Boss Rule—Portrait in City Politics*. Ayer Co. Publishers.

Smith, Adam. 2000. *The Theory of Moral Sentiments*. New York: Prometheus Books.

———. 2003. *The Wealth of Nations*. New York: Bantam Classics.

Solow, Robert M. 1956. "A Contribution to the Theory of Economic Growth." *Quarterly Journal of Economics* 70(1): 65–94.

———. 1988. *Growth Theory: An Exposition*. Oxford: Oxford University Press.

Spence, A. Michael. 1973. *Market Signalling: Information Transfer in Hiring and Related Processes*. Cambridge, MA: Harvard University Press.

Srinivasan, T.N. 1985. "Neoclassical Political Economy, the State, and Economic Development." *Asian Development Review* 3: 38–58.

Stern, Ernest H. 1944. "The Agreements of Bretton Woods." *Economica* 11(44): 165–179.

Stern, Nicholas. 1989. "The Economics of Development, A Survey." *Economic Journal* 99: 597–685.

Stevenson, R.J. 1993. "Rationality and Reality." In K.I. Manktelow and D.E. Over, eds. *Rationality, Psychological and Philosophical Perspectives*. Routledge: London and New York.

Stiglitz, Joseph. 1998. "Towards a New Paradigm for Development, Strategies, Policies, and Processes." Prebisch Lecture at UNCTAD.

———. 1999. "The World Bank at the Millennium." *Economics Journal* 109(459): F577–F597.

———. 2002. *Globalization and its Discontents*. New York: W.W. Norton & Co.

Sudgen, Robert. 1989. "Spontaneous Order." *Journal of Economic Perspectives* 3(4): 85–97.

———. 1998a. "Normative Expectations: The Simultaneous Evolution of Institutions and Norms." In Avner Ben Ner and Louis Putterman, eds. *Economics, Values, and Organization*. Cambridge: Cambridge University Press.

———. 1998b. "Spontaneous Order." *New Palgrave's Dictionary of Economics and Law*. New York: St. Martin's Press.

Tian, Garry Gang. 1997. "The FDI-Led Growth Hypothesis: Further Econometric Evidence from China." Working Paper 97/2. National Center for Developmental Studies, Australian National University.

Tirole, Jean. 1986. "Hierarchies and Bureaucracies: On the Role of Collusion in Organizations." *Journal of Law, Economics, and Organization* 2(2) (Fall): 181–214.

———. 1994. "The Internal Organization of Government." *Oxford Economic Papers* 46: 1–29.

Tocqueville, Alexis de. 2000. *Democracy in America*. Chicago: University of Chicago Press.

———. 2004. *The Old Regime and Revolution*. Vol. 1. Chicago: University of Chicago Press.

Todaro, Michael P. and Stephen C. Smith. 2002. *Economic Development*. New York: Addison Wesley.

Tullock, Gordon. 1967. "The Welfare Costs of Tariffs, Monopolies, and Theft." *Western Economic Journal* 5(3): 224–232.

United Nations Development Programme. 1998. "Good Governance and Sustainable Human Development—A Policy Document." New York: UNDP.

Vanberg, Viktor J. 1986a. "Individual Choice and Institutional Constraints: The Normative Element in Classical and Contractarian Liberalism." *Analyse & Kritik, Zeitschrift für Sozialwissenschaften* 8: 113–149.

———. 1986b. "Spontaneous Market Order and Social Rules: A Critical Examination of F.A. Hayek's Theory of Cultural Evolution." *Economics and Philosophy* 2: 75–100.

———. 1988. " 'Ordnungstheorie' as Constitutional Economics: The German Conception of a 'Social Market Economy.' " *ORDO* 39: 17–31.

———. 1993. "Constitutionally Constrained and Safeguarded Competition in Markets and Politics with Reference to a European Constitution." *Journal des Economistes et des Etudes Humaines* 4: 3–27.

———. 1994. "Cultural Evolution, Collective Learning, and Constitutional Design." In D. Reisman, ed. *Economic Thought and Political Theory*. Kluwer Academic Publishers: Boston-Dordrecht-London.

———. 2004. "The Status Quo in Contractarian-Constitutionalist Perspective," *Constitutional Political Economy* 15: 153–170.

Vanberg, Viktor J. and Wolfgang Kerber. 1994. "Institutional Competition Among Jurisdictions: An Evolutionary Approach." *Constitutional Political Economy* 5: 193–219.

Van de Walle, Nicolas. 1999. "Economic Reform in a Democratizing Africa." *Comparative Politics* 10: 21–41.

———. 2000. *The Politics of Permanent Crisis: Managing African Economies, 1979–1999*. Draft book ms. East Lansing: Michigan State University.

———. 2001. *African Economies and the Politics of Permanent Crisis, 1979–1999*. New York: Cambridge University Press.

Van de Walle, Nicolas and Timothy A. Johnston. 1996. *Improving Aid to Africa*. Washington, DC: Overseas Development Council.

Vaughn, Karen I. 1991. *Austrian Economics in America; the Migration of a Tradition*. Cambridge: Cambridge University Press.

Wade, Robert. 1985. "The Market for Public Office: Why the Indian State is not Better at Development." *World Development* 13(4): 467–497.

Wagner, Richard E. 1993. *Parchment, Guns, and Constitutional Order*. London: Edward Elgar.

———. 2002. "Complexity, Governance, and Constitutional Craftsmanship." *American Journal of Economics and Sociology* 61: 101–117.

Washington Post. 2004. "Grappling with State Failure." June 9: A20.

WCED (World Commission on Environment and Development). 1987. *Our Common Future*. New York: Oxford University Press.

Weber, Max. 1958. *Essays in Sociology*. New York: Oxford University Press.

Weimer, W.B. 1982. "Hayek's Approach to the Problems of Complex Phenomena: An Introduction to the Theoretical Psychology of *The Sensory Order*." In W.B. Weimer and D.S. Palermo, eds. *Cognition and the Symbolic Processes* Vol. 2. Hillsdale, NJ: Lawrence Erlbaum Associates.

White, Howard. 1992. "The Macro-Economic Impact of Development Aid: A Critical Survey." *Journal of Development Studies* 21(2): 163–240.

———, ed. 1998. *Aid and Macroeconomic Performance*. London: Macmillan Press.

———. 1999. *Dollars, Dialogue and Development. An Evaluation of Swedish Programme Aid*. Stockholm: Sida.

Willgerodt, Hans and Alan Peacock. 1989. "German Liberalism and Economic Revival." In A. Peacock and H. Willgerodt, eds. *Germany's Social Market Economy*: 1–14.

Williams, D.G. 1996. "Governance and the Discipline of Development." *The European Journal of Development Research* 8(2): 157–177.

Williamson, Oliver E. 1967. "Hierarchical Control and Optimum Firm Size." *Journal of Political Economy* 75(2): 123–138.

———. 1973. "Markets and Hierarchies: Some Elementary Considerations." *American Economic Review* 63(2) (May): 316–325.

———. 1995. "The Institutions and Governance of Economic Development and Reform." In Michael Bruno and Boris Pleskovic, eds. *Proceedings of the World Bank Annual Conference on Development Economics, 1994*. Washington, DC: World Bank.

Wilson, Maureen G. and Elizabeth Whitmore. 1995. "Accompanying the Process: Principles for International Development Practice." *Canadian Journal of Development Studies* (Special Issue): 61–77.

Wilson, Woodrow. 1887. "The Study of Administration." *Political Science Quarterly* 2: 197–222.

———. 1981. *Congressional Government, A Study in American Politics*. Baltimore: Johns Hopkins University Press.

Wiseman, Jack. 1990. "Principles of Political Economy: An Outline Illustrated by Application to Fiscal Federalism." *Constitutional Political Economy* 1(1): 101–124.

World Bank. 1989a. *Sub-Saharan Africa: From Crisis to Sustainable Growth*. Washington, DC: World Bank.

———. 1989b. *A Framework for Capacity-Building in Policy Analysis and Economic Management in Sub-Saharan Africa*. Washington, DC: World Bank.

———. 1991. *Proceedings of the World Bank Annual Conference*. Ed. Lawrence H. Summers and Sekhar Shah. Washington, DC: World Bank.

———. 1992. *Governance and Development*. Washington, DC: World Bank.

———. 1997. *World Development Report 1997: The State in a Changing World*. Oxford: Oxford University Press.

———. 1998. *Assessing Aid: What Works, What Doesn't and Why*. Written by David Dollar and Lant Pritchett. Oxford, UK: Oxford University Press.

———. 2002. *World Development Report: Building Institutions for Markets*. Washington, DC: World Bank.

Wunsch, James. 2000. "African Political Reform and International Assistance: What Can and Should Be Done?" In Stuart S. Segel, ed. *Handbook of Global Political Policy*. New York: Marcel Dekker.

Zachariah, Fareed. 2004. *The Future of Freedom, Illiberal Democracy at Home and Abroad*. New York: W.W. Norton & Co.

Index